THE QUEST
FOR IDENTITY
in so-called
Mainline Churches
in South Africa

EDITORS
Ernst M. Conradie
&
John Klaasen

SERIES EDITOR
Renier Koegelenberg

SUN PRESS

**EFSA
SERIES** | ECUMENICAL AND
DEVELOPMENT PERSPECTIVES

The Quest for Identity in so-called Mainline Churches in South Africa

Published by SUN MeDIA Stellenbosch under the SUN PRESS imprint.

Copyright © 2014 EFSA and authors

First edition 2014

ISBN 978-1-920689-22-3 (print)
ISBN 978-1-920689-23-0 (epub)

Set in 10.5/13 Palatino Linotype
Typesetting and conversion: SUN MeDIA Stellenbosch

SUN PRESS is an imprint of SUN MeDIA Stellenbosch. Academic, professional and reference works are published under this imprint in print and electronic format. This publication may be ordered directly from www.sun-e-shop.co.za.

Produced by SUN MeDIA Stellenbosch.

www.africansunmedia.co.za
www.sun-e-shop.co.za

Ecumenical Foundation of Southern Africa (EFSA)

Executive Chairperson, Prof. H. Russel Botman
Executive Director, Dr Renier A. Koegelenberg
Postal address: P.O. Box 3103, Matieland, Stellenbosch, 7602, South Africa
Physical address: 24-26 Longifolia Street, Paradyskloof, Stellenbosch

Office of the Executive Director
Phone: +27 (0)21 880-1734
Fax: +27 (0)21 880-1735
Fax: +27 (0)86 768-4121
Mobile: +27 (0)83 625-1047
E-mail: efsa@cddc.co.za
Websites: http://www.efsa-institute.org.za
http://www.nrasd.org.za

ACKNOWLEDGEMENTS

EFSA gratefully acknowledges the following institutions for their support of this publication:

- Die Evangelische Kirche in Deutschland (EKD)
- Brot für die Welt
- University of the Western Cape, Department of Religion and Theology

EFSA

INSTITUTE FOR THEOLOGICAL & INTERDISCIPLINARY RESEARCH

Ecumenical Foundation of Southern Africa (EFSA)

The EFSA Institute, founded in 1990, is an independent ecumenical institute that functions as a division of the non-profitable "Cape Development and Dialogue Centre Trust" (CDDC). Trustees include Dr Welile Mazamisa, Archbishop Dr Thabo Makgoba, Dr André van Niekerk, Prof. Russel Botman and Dr Renier Koegelenberg. It consists of a unique network of participating institutions: representatives of the Faculties of Theology and the Departments of Religious Studies of the Universities in the Western Cape are represented on the Board and Executive of the EFSA Institute.

Generally speaking, the EFSA Institute attempts to promote consensus between different sectors, interest groups and stakeholders on the challenges and problems facing our society. It strives to play a facilitating role by providing a platform for public debate, even of controversial issues.

Both in its structure and function there is a dialectic tension between an academic (research-based) approach and the need to address specific needs of the church and other religious communities. This tension is embedded in the main issues facing the churches in our society. In a general sense the EFSA Institute tries to focus public attention (and the attention of the church or academic institutions) on specific problems in society.

Currently, the focus is on the following priorities.

Firstly, the *development role of the church* and other religious communities: the eradication of poverty in South Africa; the role of religious networks in community development, in social and welfare services; and the development of community and youth leadership.

Secondly, the *healing and reconciliatory role of the church* and other religious communities: this includes a project on the role of women in the healing of our violent society; the mobilisation of the church and religious communities against crime and violence; and the breaking down of stereotypes (racism) in our society.

Thirdly, the *formation of values in the strengthening of a moral society by the church* and other religious communities: the promotion of moral values such as honesty; support for the weak; respect for life and human rights.

Fourthly, the *development of youth and community leadership*: special courses for the development of leadership skills among our youth have been developed and are presented to support the building of a new society.

It is also significant that the EFSA Institute acts as Secretariat to the National Religious Association for Social Development (NRASD), which is a Principal Recipient of the Global Fund to Fight AIDS, Tuberculosis and Malaria in South Africa. It is also a partner of Johns Hopkins Health and Education in South Africa (JHHESA – a USAID funded programme). It currently serves as the national secretariat of the religious sector – for the South African National Aids Council (SANAC).

These priorities cannot be separated from one another, since many of the complex social issues are interrelated.

Dr Renier A Koegelenberg
Executive Director

CONTENTS

1

WHY THE QUEST FOR IDENTITY?

Ernst Conradie

Ecumenical studies and social ethics

The Department of Religion and Theology at the University of the Western Cape is hosting a series of think tanks and public conferences on the interface between ecumenical theology and social ethics in the (South) African context. It has identified a number of critically important themes where some degree of clarity may aid further ecumenical discourse. These think tanks are being hosted over a three-year period from October 2012 to June 2015. Reflections emerging from these think tanks will be published in a series of booklets, where appropriate. The themes that are envisaged include the following:

- Guiding visions for the transition to a post-apartheid society (held November 2012);
- A critical assessment of "reconciliation" as one of the guiding visions during and beyond the transition period (held October 2012);
- Notions and forms of "ecumenicity" in (South) Africa (held February 2013);
- The quest for denominational identity within mainline churches (held May 2013);
- Ecumenical engagement in the form of NGOs and FBOs as dynamos for social transformation in the Western Cape (held August 2013);
- Religion and moral formation towards responsible citizenship (held August 2013);
- Recognising current ecclesial reform/deform movements in South Africa;
- African Pentecostal expressions of ecumenicity in (South) Africa;
- African notions of leadership;
- Ecclesiology and ethics in the (South) African context: How are ecumenical studies related to social ethics?

This series of think tanks and public conferences walks on two legs, namely ecumenical theology and social ethics, shifting the weight from one leg to the other each semester. The first think tank that addressed ecumenical theology raised the very basic question of "Notions and forms of ecumenicity" from within the South African context.

The contributions included in this volume derive from a public conference held on Friday 24 May 2013 at the University of the Western Cape on the topic "The Quest for Identity in Mainline Churches in South Africa". The speakers on the programme for this conference included Prof. John de Gruchy, who introduced the theme, and a number of very senior church leaders, namely Archbishop Stephen Brislin (Roman Catholic Church), Archbishop Thabo Makgoba (Anglican Church of Southern Africa), Bishop Musawenkosi Biyela (Evangelical Lutheran Church of Southern Africa), Rev. Jerry Pillay (President of the World Communion of Reformed Churches), Rev. Peter Storey (former presiding bishop of the Methodist Church of Southern Africa) and Rev. Lindsay Rinquest (President of the Cape Town Baptist Seminary) The observation that these invited church leaders are all male prompted some debate. The Department of Religion and Theology decided that this reflects ecclesial realities in South Africa and should be made overt. In order to allow for a gender balance, various women who are also in positions of church leadership were invited to offer responses to the contributions included in this volume. On this basis two such contributions are included here, namely by Dr Mary-Anne Plaatjies-Van Huffel (the most recent Moderator of the Cape Synod of the Uniting Reformed Church in Southern Africa) and by Dr Vicentia Kgabe (Archdeacon of the Anglican Church of Southern Africa).

The ecumenical movement and the so-called mainline churches

The theme of this volume calls for further clarification. It is crucial to note the critical edge in the way in which the theme has been conceptualised. This is not merely related to the debate on the problematic term "mainline" churches – as pointed out by John de Gruchy in his contribution. The deeper problem is that the ecumenical movement is dominated by such "mainline" churches and that the ecumenical movement itself, at least in

South Africa, seems unable to bridge the divide between such mainline churches (grouped together) and a range of independent churches, including African Instituted Churches (AICs), Pentecostal Churches (some of which have become regarded as "established" churches) and neo-Pentecostal churches. One may even argue that the ecumenical movement was born from and responded to the quest for identity amongst mainline churches. This recognition prompted the formulation of the conference theme – which is therefore deliberately one-sided. This will be balanced by a similar conference planned for 2014, which will investigate the involvement (or lack thereof) of Pentecostal churches in the ecumenical movement.

The distinctions between Christian denominations are mainly derived from a history in Europe that still affects us in South Africa today, for better or for worse. In rudimentary form, the denominational history of Christianity in South Africa may be told (and lamented!) in the following four phases:

- The establishment of various mainline denominations derived from church schisms in Europe, all trying to become deeply rooted in South Africa, yet retaining their historical ties with a particular confessional tradition and therefore sensing the need to establish their own identities in relation to each other;
- Attempts at ecumenical collaboration and fellowship to overcome such denominational divides on mission, liturgy, theological education and, of course, the struggle against apartheid and for democracy in South Africa, eventually leading to the formation of the now dormant South African Council of Churches with its 26 member churches;
- Various early and subsequent breakaway movements from such "mainline" churches –sometimes over issues of indigenous leadership (the so-called "Ethiopian"-type churches), sometimes resulting from Pentecostal renewal movements going back to 1906, sometimes the result of both these variables (including Zionist Churches) and, more recently the emergence of a host of neo-Pentecostal or "store front" churches, typically blending these breakaway movements in an urban African environment;
- The current constellation of denominational allegiance that defies easy classification in opinions polls, but where the divides between mainline churches which maintain ecumenical fellowship with each other, AICs

and Pentecostal churches are not only obvious but also open to political opportunism.

It is anyone's guess how many denominations there are in South Africa, but the very term is no longer very helpful, given the myriad of independent Pentecostal or neo-Pentecostal congregations that maintain only a very loose affiliation with other such congregations. As a result the difference between a "church", a "congregation" and a "denomination" is no longer clear.

This situation poses a serious problem for understanding ecumenical relations. One may argue that breakaway movements from mainline churches emerged as a result of dissatisfaction regarding the (lack of) rootedness of churches in Africa and in overcoming denominational divides imported from Europe. By contrast, the ecumenical movement is a response to such dissatisfaction from within the so-called mainline churches, but then in such a way that denominational identity is not compromised. This suggests that the tension between the ecumenical movement (predominantly involving so-called mainline churches) and independent churches is one that will not be overcome easily. The so-called mainline churches will find it difficult to persuade independent churches that the reasons why they broke away from the mainline churches in the first place and/or the reasons why new churches were established are less important than the need for continuity, mutual recognition and fellowship amongst all churches.

There have been several attempts by ecumenical bodies, especially by the Christian Institute and the Institute for Contextual Theology, to build bridges between the ecumenical movement and AICs. Given the brief history sketched above, it should come as no surprise that attempts to expand the ecumenical movement to include indigenous and Pentecostal church are bound to meet with resistance. After all, there were reasons why these breakaways occurred in the first place, so that attempts at inclusion if not incorporation would necessarily raise suspicions. Such suspicions were well articulated in the question posed by Rev. Thami Ximiya (from the Ethiopian Episcopal Church) during a class on ecumenical theology in Africa at UWC in 2013: "Why do you want to talk to us now?" In other words: Are leaders of mainline churches envious of the growth of AICs and Pentecostal churches? Are they trying to survive because members are drifting away from mainline churches? Are they looking for money? Why is there such a lack of interest in ecumenical gatherings, while other church gatherings can attract tens of thousands of participants?

The focus of this particular volume is not so much on such deep divides between so-called mainline churches, AICs and Pentecostal churches. That remains very much part of the agenda and will be followed up in the project on ecumenical studies and social ethics, as indicated above. Instead, the focus is on those so-called mainline churches that participate in the ecumenical movement and are member churches of the South African Council of Churches. Amongst such churches one finds, on the one hand, a recognition of the need to overcome denominational divides imported from Europe. On the other hand, there is also a constant need to explain why these denominational identities are maintained. If such identities are defined differentially (i.e. in terms of the differences), the particular identity needs ongoing clarification. At the same time, it is clear that such denominational identities have become deeply entrenched and embraced. After two or three generations of Christian adherence, the way in which things are done is simply taken for granted. That applies to all the building blocks of Christian and denominational identity, including forms of ecclesial governance, narratives, rituals, ethos, religious experience and doctrine.

The underlying question

What exactly does it mean to be a Roman Catholic, an Anglican, a Lutheran, a Reformed, a Methodist or a Baptist Christian? What is the difference between these churches at an experiential level? These differences have been internalised, embodied and practised in South Africa over many generations, so that members have come to regard them as significant for their own identity. However, upon reflection they may well find it difficult to explain to themselves what is at stake. Why should such denominational identities then be maintained? Why does it seem that ecumenical relationships are waning while there is a stronger sense of denominational identity?

This quest for identity is radicalised in the light of what may be called a "branded Christianity", where churches compete with each other in the market of providing religious services and attracting adherents. Understandably, many mainline churches fear losing their members to other churches or to secularism, with serious financial implications. One may wish to resist such a "branded Christianity" by insisting on the need for ecumenical fellowship and thus underplay the differences, but this only underlines the need to clarify denominational identity. Why exactly is that still important?

Each of the contributors from the six selected confessional traditions was asked to address the following questions:

> What continues to attract people to the church and what are the issues that they struggle with in terms of distinguishing such identity in relation to other so-called mainline denominations, Pentecostal and independent/indigenous churches, other religious traditions and secular ways of life? Why maintain denominational identities? What is at stake?

This may appear to be something akin to an ecclesial beauty contest, but the existential nature of the question within mainline churches is undeniable. In a recent survey of postgraduate theses completed in the Department of Religion and Theology, it was striking to see to what extent this question is addressed in numerous manifestations by UWC students. There is, of course, also considerable interest in responding to societal issues such as economic justice, social cohesion, democracy, violence against women, HIV/AIDS, and environmental destruction. These are related to ecumenical concerns in the field of "ethics", which has dominated ecumenical debates, at least in South Africa. However, the ecumenical concerns over issues of "ecclesiology" continue to simmer and become evident in the quest for identity in those so-called mainline churches that are members of the World Council of Churches and the South African Council of Churches.

The particular focus of this volume is therefore relativised from the outset as only one aspect of a larger agenda. Nevertheless, it is one that requires attention for the sake of honesty and integrity, and given the lasting impact of denominationalism in South Africa. Each of the contributions indicates to what extent confessional identities have become internalised, embodied and practised in South Africa.

Ernst Conradie is Senior Professor in the Department of Religion and Theology at the University of the Western Cape.

2

THE QUEST FOR IDENTITY IN THE SO-CALLED "MAINLINE" CHURCHES IN SOUTH AFRICA

John W de Gruchy

The quest for identity is the search for self-understanding. How do the so-called "mainline" churches understand themselves? The quest also has to do with how others understand them. How do other churches who do not regard themselves as "mainline" understand them? How do people of other faith traditions understand them? How do those in government, trade union leaders, academics and business people understand them? How does the proverbial "man in the street" understand them? And, not least, how do those who belong to these churches understand themselves? Identity has to do with image, the way in which we communicate who we are, the way in which the media represent us, and therefore the way in which others relate to us. As such, the quest for identity is inseparable from our reason for existence, and therefore in the case of the churches, their task or mission.

I will approach the subject in two parts. The first has to do with deconstructing the accumulated identities the so-called mainline churches already have, whether in popular or academic discourse in South Africa, or the confessional identities they represent in our context. The second has to do with their present quest for identity, the identities that are currently being constructed, or identities in the making.

1. Deconstructing accumulated identities

All the so-called "mainline" churches in South Africa are part of world-wide confessional families, whether Anglican, Lutheran, Baptist, Reformed or Methodist. This is the identity they have inherited, an identity with a range of distinctive features which are both local and global. This identity has strengthened not diminished in recent times, as confessional families have developed and clarified their own identities in relation to others. So the so-called "mainline" churches in South Africa today not only share origins, history, faith, spirituality and practice (whether ethical or liturgical) with global partners, but they continue to develop their confessional identities through worldwide dialogue, aided greatly by modern means of communication and transport (see Meyer & Vischer 1984). The Roman Catholic Church, when identified as a "mainline" church, does not think of itself in precisely these terms, but there are family resemblances and, of course, all the "mainline" churches originally stem from the same Western Catholic tradition. These confessional identities are the substratum of all subsequent accumulated identities that define the "mainline" churches in South Africa.

These confessional roots were first planted in a very different context to that in which the "mainline" churches now exist. They are no longer churches in Europe but churches in South Africa. As a result, their confessional identities and the discourse associated with them does not always or easily connect to the vast majority of the membership of these churches today, whose cultural background and experience of being the church may be different. This will vary in degree from one church to the next, with Roman Catholics having a greater sense of universal identity and conformity than others. But black Lutherans, for example, especially lay people as distinct from the theologically trained, are generally not copycats of German Lutherans any more than are the equivalents in any of the other churches. The result is that although these churches have a confessional identity, it may sometimes be a veneer placed on top of a more meaningful and immediate sense of being Christian and being the church in South Africa. Many members are less interested in the confessional identity of their churches, except as names that distinguish them from others, and more interested in whether or not their local congregation provides a meaningful home, and whether or not their church is truly serving their needs.

Quite apart from their denominational or confessional identities, the so-called "mainline" churches in South Africa have been variously known and described over the past century in attempts to identify them collectively (see De Gruchy & De Gruchy 2004:1-50). They have been referred to, inter alia, as settler, colonial, mission, multiracial and the ecumenical churches. "Settler" refers to their planting in South Africa as a result of European immigration; "colonial" refers to their relationship to the colonial enterprise and to the colonial authorities with whom they generally had a cosy relationship; "mission" refers to the fact that each of them began extensive missionary programmes amongst indigenous peoples to such an extent that today they have become black majority churches; and "multiracial" describes their ethnic composition in more recent times. The designation "ecumenical" has been used since the 1980s, because the majority of these churches have been members of the World Council and the South African Council of Churches and participated in other ecumenical structures and initiatives. The fact that these designations are often prefaced by the words "so-called" indicates how inadequate these terms are as indicators of identity.

There is another set of inherited identities, one that reflects divisions within historic settler society, namely the Afrikaans Reformed churches and the English-speaking churches. For many, these identities have been paramount, and for some they still are. Much can and has been said about these two groups of churches in terms of their identities. We cannot go into that complex story now. But to illustrate some of the issues involved in the quest for identity let me say something about the so-called English-speaking churches by reference to the Church Unity Commission.

When the Church Unity Commission (CUC) was established in 1967, the then Archbishop of Cape Town, Robert Selby Taylor, invited leaders of most of the "mainline" churches to participate in what was phrased as the "search for church unity" in Southern Africa. Six churches responded to his invitation, including his own: the Methodist Church of Southern Africa, the Presbyterian Church of Southern Africa, the Evangelical or Tsonga Presbyterian Church, the Reformed or Bantu Presbyterian Church and the United Congregational Church of Southern Africa. The Lutheran

Federation (FELCSA) requested observer status, as did the Roman Catholic Church, while the rest of those invited decided not to participate in any way. Leaders of the participating CUC churches already knew each other through ecumenical structures, and the CUC mirrored other talks about church unity in Britain and in other formerly British colonies. So the formation of the CUC was a logical step forward in the ecumenical movement, even though it transcended confessional identities: Anglican, Methodist and Reformed.

As a result of the work of the CUC, there are now a number of united congregations around the country as well as an acknowledgement of each other's ministry that is well in advance of what has been achieved in most other countries.[1] Even though "organic union" has been elusive and is no longer the major intention of the CUC, members of these churches generally have little difficulty in moving from one to the other as personal circumstances change. But the designation "English-speaking churches" is an anachronism today, given the constituency of these churches. As Secretary of the CUC during its first five years (1968-1973), I became acutely aware that while church unity issues primarily centred around matters of "faith and order", this was largely a white European preoccupation. Black participants rightly insisted that church unity had more to do with overcoming racial segregation in the church than uniting English-speaking white-led denominations. Uniting churches without their transformation would not make any difference either to the churches themselves or to the plight of their members in an apartheid society. This forced us to recognise that the unity of the church was not simply a matter of uniting structures previously divided on the basis of a common confession of faith; it was as much about its common witness in the world. To be united in the struggle against apartheid was as important as, or even more important than, uniting the churches in one institutional body.

---

1   See *Journal of Theology for Southern Africa* 23 (June 1978), which includes the Proposed Covenant and articles on related themes. The Covenant, formerly adopted that year, also led to the mutual acceptance not only of membership but also of each other's ordained ministry, thereby making it possible for ministers of each participating church to serve in the other participating churches.

To speak of the English- or Afrikaans-speaking churches today may serve some purpose, but the terms are hopefully being consigned to the past as new ecumenical links are being forged both within and between confessional structures. The changes that have occurred in South Africa since the early 1990s have resulted, for example, in greater dialogue and cooperation between the Dutch Reformed family of churches and the other so-called "mainline" churches. Hence the emergence of a new identity, namely "mainline", to describe them. But does this new branding have any theological and ecclesiological significance, or is it simply a convenient label used in a derogatory way by those who regard the historical denominations as dead, and sometimes in a triumphalist way by those who regard these churches as the only true representative/s of the "one, holy, catholic and apostolic church"?

The term "mainline" originally referred to a train line in the city of Philadelphia in the United States that separated more wealthy neighbourhoods from more recent, and poorer, immigrant communities. The former attended churches that had long been established; the latter were mainly Irish and Italian Roman Catholics. But in more recent times the term has become widely used in America to describe those major Protestant denominations that were dominant in the country until towards the last decades of the twentieth century in contrast to new Pentecostal, fundamentalist, charismatic and independent churches which have grown rapidly to the extent that they have now, collectively, overtaken the "mainline churches".[2] Generally speaking the "mainline" churches in the USA are more theologically and politically liberal, more engaged in social justice issues, more ecumenical in outlook, more willing to engage in interfaith dialogue, largely white in membership, and exclusively Protestant. It is widely held by the "non-mainline" Protestant churches that their decline is due to the fact that they have departed from their original conservative evangelical character.

Those churches in South Africa that are historically or confessionally connected to the "mainline" Churches in North America are similarly

---

2   The literature on the subject is vast. See e.g. Hutcheson (1981) and McKinney (1998).

understood by other churches in the country. The result is that the image of the "mainline" churches that has developed there has been transposed onto the South African scene, as it has also in Britain and elsewhere in ways that are often inappropriate. Commenting on the use of the term in Britain, Keith Clements, the British Baptist theologian and ecumenical leader, expresses his unease with the description. Not only are Roman Catholics usually included in the term in Britain, but many of the "newer" churches, he says, are actually part of the "main stream" (e.g. black Pentecostal or other black-led churches), and many of the "emergent" churches are in fact offshoots with continuing links to "mainline" churches. It is, he says, "a very blurry scene right now".[3] There are similar problems with the use of the term in South Africa which make it less than helpful as a description. Not least amongst them is that the so-called "mainline" churches in South Africa are predominantly black in membership and their theologies vary considerably. They simply have a different history and ethos, despite their similarities with their American counterparts.

One of the obvious and more substantive problems with using the term "mainline" wherever it is used is that it suggests that some churches are inferior to others; it side-lines them as it did when originally used in Philadelphia. They are, as it were, on the wrong side of the railway tracks. As such the term can lead to a triumphalist attitude on the part of some and resentment on the part of others. The "mainline" churches are, so it suggests, those churches with the best pedigrees, the ones who best represent the Christian church in South Africa. But the truth is that in the course of our histories we have all been side-lined by others who claimed to be "mainline", even if that term is of recent vintage. In any case, is not the term "mainline" indicative of being too closely identified with political power? Some of us now tagged "mainline" feel more comfortable in dissent from establishment rather than being part of it. Are there no other churches that have, in fact, become "mainline" in this sense? And where, for example, do the Orthodox Churches, whether Greek or Coptic, fit into such a description? In sum, the term "mainline" is a hindrance not a help in our quest to be the church of Jesus Christ in southern Africa.

---

3   Correspondence of Keith Clements with John de Gruchy, 30 April 2013.

I specifically refer to *southern* Africa because most of the "mainline" churches in South Africa describe themselves in this way. This means that their quest for identity cannot be confined to one nation, country, and certainly not one ethnic group if the labels we use indicate otherwise; it is a quest that transcends national and tribal boundaries with all that this means in terms of culture, politics, history and the future. The church of Jesus Christ cannot be reduced to a *Volkskerk* or "national church" in the sense that the Church of England, the Church of Denmark, or the Russian Orthodox Church have historically claimed to be and still are in different ways. The struggle of the Anglican Church in Southern Africa, which began with the heated debate over Bishop John Colenso in the nineteenth century, to distance itself from the colonial authorities and enterprise has been part of its quest for its own authentic identity in this context, which has in turn reshaped the identity of the worldwide Anglican Communion.

There is more than a linguistic issue at stake when we use the preposition "of" instead of "in". Can the church ever be the church *of* South or Southern Africa? Theologically speaking, the church can only be the church *of* Jesus Christ which exists *in* South Africa or wherever else it exists. Theologically speaking, there can be no Church *of* England or *of* South Africa. The church can never be confined to or equated with a particular nation without losing something fundamental to its identity as the church of Jesus Christ. Thus we must always resist the perennial designs of political power to co-opt the church for its own purposes.

In fact, one of the key issues that has shaped the identities of all the so-called "mainline" churches, whether Catholic or Protestant, has to do with the way in which these churches have sought to relate to political power. This has often been a major source of contention and division, for some have been national churches whether officially or in fact, and others have struggled against being such. That is why some ecclesial traditions were historically labelled non-conformist or "free church". But they are no longer divided by such issues, because none are state churches in South Africa; they are all free churches, even if they do not describe themselves as such.

Even though the role of the so-called "mainline" churches in the struggle against apartheid varied and the record is not all that positive, there is a sense in which those dubbed the "ecumenical churches" discovered a common identity in that struggle (see De Gruchy 2002). That has been an important stage in their quest for identity as churches in southern Africa. In the same way, their attempt to witness prophetically to the state and speak truth to power today is an important indicator of their common quest for identity. They are learning together to negotiate the boundaries between being church and being part of a new nation, and so develop a relevant understanding of, and discourse about, church-state relations in a new context. In doing so they can draw on a common legacy that goes back over many centuries in which church-state relations were forged in Europe, and reformulated in apartheid South Africa. They therefore have some experience and understanding of their strengths and weaknesses, and as such they have a framework for relating to political authority today (see Barth 1960:101-148; Yoder 1964; Abbott 1966).

This, I suggest, is not as true of some of the "newer" denominations in South Africa which – if they are seriously and theologically working out their own approaches to the issues and not just responding pragmatically – are more influenced by the church-state debates and controversies in recent American history. This may be one reason why the so-called "mainline" churches relate to the state differently to some of the other church groups who do not have that history, experience, or theology of church-state relations. They do not talk from the same script, as it were. But it is important that they do not forget what they have learnt about how the church should relate to political power and not be tempted to be seduced by it.

2. Identities in the making

The identity of churches should neither be reduced to historical, sociological and media descriptions, nor solely determined by their confessional origins and history; if that was all that could be said about them, they would be trapped in our past and unable to move together into the future in South Africa. So let us now consider the quest for identity as an ecumenical process in which churches discern together where they are being led by the Holy Spirit today.

The New Testament scholar Paul Minear once wrote about the flexible imagination of the early Christians in thinking about the identity of the church. It was flexible, he wrote, "because it was so alive to the mystery of the church's participation in the creative and redemptive work of the Triune God. Perception of this mystery induced an almost endless variety of modes of describing it" (Minear 1960:250). Yet, Minear continued, "if we are to believe the cumulative witness of the New Testament, every congregation was all too prone to blindness. It did not see itself either as it was or as it was meant to become."

Symptomatic of this blindness is the fact that we too often speak about and think of "our" churches as denominations rather than the church of Jesus Christ. This may reflect an appropriate modesty on the part of some.[4] But it can also lead to the opposite, whereby a denomination regards itself as *the* church in isolation from others. The justifications for doing so, just as the original reasons given for division, are many, but they are invariably self-justifications to demonstrate that some are the true church and others less so (Evans 1994:130-139). Incidentally, the word "denomination" has no theological significance; it is a sociological term which refers to the disintegration and fragmentation of the Christian church over the centuries, as differences led to divisions in the church with rival claims of some to be the true church over against others (see Niebuhr 1957). Denominationalism is a mindset that regards the denomination as an end in itself. As such, it is sectarian.

Unfortunately, much talk about the identity of churches today takes us back into our denominational comfort zones, or what *we* want the church to be. In his recent book *Ecumenical Dynamic*, Keith Clements (2013:198) makes an important observation:

> A major feature of the church scene today is the growing preoccupation of churches and denominations with their own

---

4   See the report on the Church in the United States by Dietrich Bonhoeffer (1998:434-445).

identity, the search by each for a secure plot on which to build their designer-home in what they think is their distinctive and unique architecture of the spirit.

Clements goes on to speak of the danger of churches being obsessed by the problem of their own identity, of discovering who they are, because it can become a way of avoiding being in relation to others within the church of Jesus Christ as a whole. That is why the quest for the identity of the church must always be an ecumenical quest; when it is not, it is inevitably sectarian (Evans 1994:121-173). Unless churches want to be sectarian, they need to break out of thinking denominationally about their identity and consider themselves, divided as they are, as members one of another in the church of Jesus Christ. Even the attempt to try and establish their own particular identity first as a platform to engage others is a denial of the fact that they can only discover who they are in relation to the church as a whole, and they can only become more truly what they are meant to be as they journey with others.

Not long ago I was asked to chair a meeting of the doctrine committee of the Church Unity Commission. I proposed at the outset that each participant should talk not about what was important for their own denomination or confession, but what they valued about that of the others. This shifted the focus from the defence or praise of one's own tradition to an appreciation of what others contribute to the life and witness of the church. Too often we see ourselves in competition, pointing out the weaknesses and failures of others while promoting and lauding our own strengths and achievements. Too often we relate to others on the basis of stereotypes, whether intentionally or not.

My own life as a Christian and a human being has been immeasurably enriched as a result of a lifetime of ecumenical involvement and engagement. I treasure my Reformed and Congregational tradition and ethos, but I am undoubtedly an ecumenical hybrid. This is the experience of many people around the world today who speak of an "emerging church" that is transgressing denominational boundaries and transcending inherited stereotypes (see, inter alia, McLaren 2004). This is a necessary and healthy reaction to both denominationalism and to a faltering ecumenical movement, but only so long as it does not become yet another denomination. At the first Conference of Faith and Order, held in Lausanne, Switzerland, in 1927, one of the participants, Peter Ainslie, a leader within the Disciples of Christ (which came into being in an attempt to unite Protestant Churches in the United States but sadly ended up creating a new one), made this statement:

> My denomination must grow less in my eyes if I am to grow more towards Christ. I am willing that my denomination shall be forgotten if thereby may be hastened the unity of the Church of our Lord. That denomination is most prophetic that is willing to disappear for Christ's sake – to go to its disappearance as deliberately as Christ went to his crucifixion (in Bate 1927:343).

Not many of us might relish the idea of *our* denomination going out of business, but in seeking to become more truly the church of Jesus Christ rather than our own possession, this may be a necessary part of the journey into God's future. At best, denominational structures are interim measures enabling us to bear witness to certain insights and embody certain gifts of God that have been forgotten or lost. But even in doing so, we need to recognise the insights and gifts inherent in other traditions, and accept them as belonging to us all. They are no church's inherent right or possession, but God requires us to share them with each other. In other words, we need to develop a sense of identity that transcends denominationalism and confessionalism. With this in mind, let us take our bearings from the New Testament.

The quest for identity has been an issue for the church since its birth at Pentecost, when the first Christians had to decide whether the church should be exclusively Jewish in character or inclusive of Gentiles. The decision to become an inclusive church fundamentally changed its identity from a sect within Judaism, and set it on the path towards becoming a catholic or universal church. As such it was believed to be the embodiment of God's "new humanity" in which ethnic, class and gender divisions were transformed and reconciled. The temptation to regress to some kind of exclusive sectarian community, whether determined by nationality, ethnicity or culture, is one that has continually challenged the church through the ages, as it has done in recent times in South Africa. It is a temptation that must always be resisted in the quest for the identity of the church.

The development of the early church as an inclusive universal community of faith was not primarily of the church's own choosing; the church was launched on this path by the Spirit of Pentecost much against the will and inclination of its leaders. Even though they heatedly debated the issues, as we still do, in the end they endorsed the action of the Spirit that led them to become what they had never intended or thought possible. Their task was to discern how and where the Spirit was leading them into the future in response to God's unfolding creative and redemptive purposes in history. So, too, we today should be seeking together to understand where the Holy Spirit is leading the church in South and southern Africa today. As such, the quest for identity is a process of ecumenical discernment.

Another biblical clue to the quest for identity can be discerned in the metaphors and images used to describe the Church in the New Testament (see Minear 1960). What is of critical importance is that these are invariably Christological in character, as when, for example, the church is described as the "body of Christ". Whatever else the church might be, its identity is inseparable from Jesus Christ; it belongs to him not to us. It is Christ who gives the church its identity. The relationship between Christ and the church is fundamental to all else. If we seek the identity of the church elsewhere we are sure to go astray in doing so. The question "Who is Jesus Christ for us today?" is therefore central to our quest in discerning the identity of the Church today (see Bonhoeffer 2010:503). The church, as Dietrich Bonhoeffer (2005:97) put it, "is nothing but that piece of humanity where Christ really has taken form."

For this reason the quest for the identity of the church is about its continual formation or renewal through the Word and Spirit into conformity with the incarnate life, death and resurrection of Christ in responding to God's mission in the world (Bonhoeffer 2005:92-97). Conformity to his incarnate life means that the church is fully and truly embodied in the life of the world; but because the church belongs only to Christ, it is never of the world. Conformity to Christ's death means that the church is called to be the servant of the world not its lord, a redemptive church of grace, forgiveness and reconciliation, a church in solidarity with all who seek the wholeness of life, and especially those who suffer and are oppressed. Therefore any legalistic or triumphalist notions of identity are excluded. Conformity to the risen Christ means that the church is always a community of hope, of new life, of transformation. It is within this Christological paradigm that the identity of the church emerges as it is faithful to the leading of the Spirit in witnessing to the coming of God's reign.

The Christological inclusivity of the church does not mean that there are no boundaries to the identity of the church, as though being inclusive implies that anything and everything is embraced within its life. This was recognised by the Confessing Church in Germany during the Third Reich, when it insisted that the true church of Jesus Christ could not be a church which supported Nazism (see Bonhoeffer 1998:654-680). In the same way, some churches in South Africa drew the line in declaring that the theological justification of apartheid was a heresy and that the church could not be segregated and remain truly Christian. There are lines to be drawn, but it is equally important to remember that we do not draw them. The boundaries between church and world are drawn by Christ, not erected by us. And when Christ draws the boundary line it is to ensure that the church *is* inclusive, not nationalistic or racially segregated, a church of justice and peace, not injustice and violence. That is why there is always a tension between the church faithfully bearing witness to Christ and the unity of the church, especially in the struggle for justice (see De Gruchy 2013:2-16).

The quest for our identity as churches must always be an ecumenical quest, then, because we are seeking to discern what it means to be the church of Jesus Christ, not what it means to be a denomination or narrowly confessional. We are part of a much larger story than our own. But this does not mean there is no room for difference within the church; differences are not only inevitable, but they also enriching and renewing. Not to allow and cherish differences is the surest way to bring about division and schism. The church was never meant to be a monolithic bureaucratic institution of sameness, but a community of believers of many gifts and insights. Each so-called denomination brings something important to the quest, some insight into the gospel previously not recognised or willingly accepted, a rich history of spirituality and experience in serving the world. This is comparable to the way in which the religious orders within the Roman Catholic Church contribute to the life of the church in varying ways, with different spiritualities, theological perspectives and vocations, without destroying but rather enriching the unity of the church. One of the great achievements of the ecumenical movement is the awakening of this sense of complementarity amongst all the churches involved, whether Orthodox, Catholic or Protestant.

Divisions occur and denominations arise because this exercise of gifts is prevented and these gifts and insights denied. But we should never forget that the differences that led to schism and denominationalism were originally related to a genuine quest to be the church of Jesus Christ, not to divide the church. If the question "What does it mean to be the church of Jesus Christ?" has tragically divided the church in past times, it is also the only question that can now lead to its renewal, for despite our differences, our quest arises out of a genuine desire to serve Jesus Christ in the world. It is this desire that should shape our identity as we move towards God's future, growing together into Christ in service of the world.

The ecumenical movement truly understood is, then, the story of trying to recover that vision, the story of divided churches reimagining their identities as the church of Jesus Christ as they journey together in serving the world rather than in isolation from each other in ecclesiastical silos. It is the result of Christians and churches rediscovering themselves as being the ecumenical church through worshipping and witnessing together and so being led by the Word and Spirit deeper into Christ to discover the riches of the gospel that overflow the container that is our own denomination or tradition.

The ecumenical quest for identity therefore requires a sharing with each other of that which God has given to us for the enrichment of all, so that the church as a whole may participate more faithfully in God's mission. It requires the recognition of the "other traditions" as having integrity and authenticity within the one church of Jesus Christ. It requires an openness to listen for the truth that is being expressed, and a willingness to learn and appreciate where the "other" is coming from. It requires a willingness to be self-critical where necessary, and an acknowledgement of weakness and failure in our own Church tradition and practice. Above all else, it requires an openness to listen to what the Spirit is saying to the churches together here and now, and therefore a commitment to pray together for each other and to pray together for the world. If the Spirit is leading the church into the fullness of Christ, its identity can never be fully or only answered in terms of past history ("where we have come from") or reduced to confessional statements ("what we believe") and denominational distinctiveness ("this is how we do things"), for the quest has to do with who we are becoming as we journey into the future led by the Spirit in obedience to Christ within our historical context.

This brings us to a critical observation in thinking about our quest for identity, for it is a quest in South and southern Africa. We are churches on a journey together within the context of this sub-continent – a context plagued by poverty, violent crime and corruption, of racism and economic injustice, of crises in education, health and housing, of xenophobia, of drug addiction, and of violence against women, children and homosexuals. Our quest for identity can only be Christ-centred and led by the Spirit if it arises out of a deep concern for this world. For it is within this world that the Holy Spirit calls, prods and pushes us beyond the boundaries of our past, out of our comfort zones as denominations, to witness to God's reign. We cannot extract what we are meant to become from the concrete situation in which we now find ourselves. But together we are called to anticipate the coming of God's reign in relation to the world in which we live. It is within southern Africa and the global reality of which it is a part that we have to engage in the *missio Dei* in the strength of the Spirit. And it is in doing so that our identity as the church of Jesus Christ will become evident as it did for the early church following Pentecost.

In line with this, it is noteworthy that Pope Francis has called on the Roman Catholic Church, and by implication on all churches, to become a "church of the poor". This is not a denial of Catholic or any other confessional identity; it is giving that identity a clear and decisive mission focus within the world. Others have spoken in a similar way in calling on the church to become a prophetic church of justice, reconciliation and peace, or a church that is inclusive in its embrace of cultural and other diversities. All this is in continuity with what Bonhoeffer (2010:500) wrote about in prison when he spoke of the church only being the church of Jesus Christ when it becomes a "church for others". The failure of the church in Europe was that "Jesus" had disappeared from view. Instead of "being there for others", the church was always defending itself, afraid to take any risks (Bonhoeffer 2010:500).

Fundamental to the churches' ecumenical quest for identity, then, is their ongoing transformation through conformation to the Incarnate, Crucified and Risen Christ about which I spoke at the outset. As we seek to be faithful to that which we have received separately or together, we are also seeking to be faithful to the gospel as it speaks to us today, and to do so in anticipation of the coming reign of God's justice and peace. We cannot remain what we were, but we have not yet become what we shall be together in Christ. And it is through growing into conformity to Christ in serving the needs of the world that we actually discover one another and grow into maturity as the "body of Christ". At the end of the day, our respective ecclesial identities will be judged in terms of the extent to which they relate to the good news of Jesus Christ that speaks of God's concern for justice, compassion, healing and redemption for the world. So let us not be too bothered about seeking our identity; let us rather seek to do what God asks of us, for in doing so we will become known for who we should really be.

Bibliography

Abbott, Walter M, SJ (ed.) 1964. *The Documents of Vatican II.* London and Dublin: Geoffrey Chapman.

Barth, Karl 1960. *Community, State, and Church: Three Essays.* Garden City: Doubleday.

Bate, HN (ed.) 1927. *Faith and Order: Proceedings of the World Conference, Lausanne, August 3-21.* London: SCM.

Bonhoeffer, Dietrich 1998. "Protestantism without Reformation". In: *Illegale Theologenausbildung: Sammelvikariate 1937-1940. Dietrich Bonhoeffer Werke 15,* 434-435. München: Chr. Kaiser Verlag.

Bonhoeffer, Dietrich 2005. *Ethics, Dietrich Bonhoeffer Works 6*. Minneapolis: Fortress.

Bonhoeffer, Dietrich 2010. *Letters and Papers from Prison, Dietrich Bonhoeffer Works 8*. Minneapolis: Fortress.

Clements, Keith 2013. *Ecumenical Dynamic: Living in More than One Place at the Same Time*. Geneva: World Council of Churches.

De Gruchy, John W 2002. "From Resistance to National Reconciliation: the Response and Role of the Ecumenical Church in South Africa". In: Cooper, Kate & Gregory, Jeremy (eds): *Retribution, Repentance and Reconciliation, Studies in Church History volume 40*, 369-384. Woodbridge and Rochester: Botdell & Brewer.

De Gruchy, John W 2013. "The Tension between Confessing Christ and the Unity of the Church in the Struggle for Justice". In: Cochrane, James R et al. (eds): *Living on the Edge: Essays in Honour of Steve de Gruchy Activist & Theologian*, 2-16. Pietermaritzburg: Cluster Publications.

De Gruchy, John W with De Gruchy, Steve 2004. *The Church Struggle in South Africa, 25th Anniversary Edition*. London: SCM.

Evans, GR 1994. *The Church and the Churches: Towards an Ecumenical Ecclesiology*. Cambridge: Cambridge University Press.

Hutcheson, Richard G 1981. *Mainline Churches and the Evangelicals: A Challenging Crisis?* Atlanta: John Knox Press.

McKinney, William 1998. "Mainline Protestantism". *Annals of the American Academy of Political and Social Science* 558:57-66.

McLaren, Brian D 2004. *A Generous Orthodoxy*. Grand Rapids: Zondervan.

Meyer, Harding & Vischer, Lukas 1984. *Growth in Agreement: Reports and Agreed Statements of Ecumenical Conversations on a World Level*. New York: Paulist Press.

Minear, Paul S 1960. *Images of the Church in the New Testament*. Philadelphia: Westminster.

Niebuhr, H Richard 1957. *The Social Sources of Denominationalism*. New York: Meridien.

Yoder, John Howard 1964. *The Christian Witness to the State*. Newton: Faith and Life Press.

John de Gruchy is Emeritus Professor of Christian Studies, University of Cape Town, and Extraordinary Professor of Theology at Stellenbosch University.

3

THE QUEST FOR IDENTITY

The Roman Catholic Church

Stephen Brislin

Much could be said on the quest for identity with reference to the Roman Catholic Church, but I have confined myself to the broad shift of emphasis that has occurred in the Church, although the identity of the Church has been preserved.

The four marks of the Church

At least since the early fifth century (and embryonically even before) the identity of the church has been summed up, quite explicitly, as "one, holy, catholic and apostolic". The journey to defining those marks and the history that has shaped it has been tortuous and varied. Notwithstanding that, the Nicene Creed, which morphed into the Constantinopolitan Creed, already holds that "we believe ... and in one, holy, catholic and apostolic church".

Those marks have consistently formed the basis of the Roman Catholic Church's self-understanding over the centuries. Different eras, however, have displayed different emphases. As history and theological contro-versies posed challenges to the church's life, different emphases and responses emerged within the various marks. For example, holiness in the early church was eventually overtaken by an emphasis on unity in the medieval church. Furthermore, in the time of Francis of Assisi, not only was the contestation around holiness but also around poverty as being the authentic expression of holiness. Holiness was defined as literally obeying Jesus' call in Matthew 19:21 to sell all you have and give the money to the poor. This arose against the background of a church that had become very wealthy and indeed corrupt, in certain aspects. I am reminded of the pithy comment of the fiery preacher Girolamo Savonarola (1452-1498), who bemoaned the fact that in the early church you had bishops of gold and chalices of wood; now, he said, you have chalices of gold and bishops of wood! Yet despite the vagaries of history and its various emphases, all four marks continued to be held collectively and together shape the church's identity. Even more to the point, this dynamic showed an early understanding of the reception of credal ideas adjusting to specific circumstances or contexts.

St Thomas Aquinas comments on these marks, saying that they are based on the shared faith of members, the common hope of eternal life and the common love of God and of neighbour expressed in mutual service. Interestingly, all of this already points to a now re-emerging hermeneutic of sharing and service. It could be called a "dangerous memory", which I suggest is significant with regard to identity.

The hermeneutic of continuity

In the light of this, I want to suggest that notions of identity can best be understood through a hermeneutic of continuity – a way of understanding that our present identity and the way in which it should ordinarily spread into the future must be seen as a contextual application of the very marks that have always defined the church.

A critical mark of the church in this regard is the notion of "catholic" with its inherent sense of wholeness and unity. Teilhard de Chardin would later image this sense of wholeness and unity as a "sacrament of creation". Karl Rahner phrased it as "liturgy of the world".

The changing mode of identity

For a very long time the dominant mode of identity in the Catholic Church has been focused on "communion with and obedience to the Pope". This became the condition of membership in the one, holy, catholic and apostolic church, which reached a dramatic high point in the bull of Boniface VIII in 1302, which declared that every human creature had to be subject to the Roman Pontiff in order to be saved! (cited in Madges 2006:12).

It was in the 1960s that the Roman Catholic Church came to a point where in its own self-understanding it could understand "catholicity" more broadly and could speak of Christ's church subsisting or existing in the catholic church, but that elements of sanctification and truth are found outside its boundaries and that this should impel us to seek the unity implied in this teaching (*Lumen Gentium* 8). Building on this conciliar insight, Cardinal Avery Dulles (2006:46) reminds us: "Vatican II presents catholicity not as a monotonous repetition of identical elements but rather as a reconciled diversity. It is a unity amongst individuals and groups that retain their distinctive characteristics, who enjoy different spiritual gifts and are by their diversity better equipped to serve one another and advance the common good. Individual Christians and local churches are bound to each other in mutual service and mutual receptivity."

Thus, in *Lumen Gentium* 9 it is said that the church offers herself, positions herself, as a "lasting and sure seed of unity, hope and salvation for the whole human race".

Implications

This understanding of catholicity has several important implications.

It means that the church has ceased to be sectarian, that it resists what has sometimes been called the "sectarian impulse". It means that the church does not believe it is a church of the saved, of saints, the true believers alone. It is equally the church of pilgrims, seekers, the weak, those in whom great deposits of unbelief continue to exist. Added to this, the church does not hold that the world and its institutions are depraved. In Greek culture, in Roman law, in Gothic vitalities, in democratic institutions, in economic progress, the church sees signs of grace and the touch of God. Thus it is the vocation of the people of the church to labour and build up such institutions shaping them by degrees according to the spirit of the Gospels.

The "New Evangelisation" mooted by Pope John Paul II and continued by Pope Emeritus Benedict and Pope Francis aims precisely at shaping and transforming different sectors of society to the spirit of the Gospel, including the political, economic and cultural sectors. It is a call for a new ardour and boldness in proclaiming the Gospel, using new methods, without proselytising but nonetheless with the aim of leading people to an encounter with Christ, including those who already know Christ, but have for some reason fallen away from faith or grown apathetic. This is the task of all the baptised – to bring Christ into the public square.

Secondly, this reception of the conciliar understanding of catholicity contrasts with what is sometimes called, for want of a better term, the ethnic spirit. It states the belief that the church is composed of all groups, all peoples, all nations. It respects the incarnate nature of human life, the existence of particular people, cultures, languages, born of the peculiarities of history. The church does not ride roughshod over these particularities. It respects them, but nonetheless holds that the church is not identical to them. Linked to this is the important understanding mentioned earlier that the church also discerns the workings of grace in all cultures, in the various trajectories of history, from the very beginning. Without in any way discounting the distinctiveness of Christianity, this does mean that other religions and different ideologies have spiritual riches to teach. Faith is marked by diversity and a wonderful pluralism. Everyone has much to learn and much to teach!

From the days of the Council we have learnt, as a church, that we are called to admire, learn from and even incorporate all signs of God's love and beauty, liberty and communion amongst the world's peoples. Michael Novak (2006:49-50) says that the Catholic spirit is less a spirit of limits than it is of fullness.

The Catholic Church in South Africa

This understanding underlines the core values of solidarity and service as particularly important for our context in South Africa. The International Theological Commission's 1985 document, meant to assist local churches in understanding their contribution to society, spoke of the need to promote participation, freedom and equality. If one reads this, in alignment with what I loosely call the "Catholic impulse", we see that contextualising the mark of catholicity necessarily means that the church's self-understanding must take it to the heart of public life, a view that is reinforced by the call for the "new evangelisation".

The church in South Africa has obviously received this identity, this understanding, of catholicity within the context of the South African reality. It has shown continuity with the notions of solidarity and service referred to in the comment of Aquinas. It has also contextualised the Vatican Council's notions of catholicity.

The South African reality is defined historically by a series of losses: losses of dignity, land, family systems, cultural values and, often times, a loss of hope and a sense of wellbeing. The legacy of the past continues to weigh heavily on the present and in many ways still defines the present.

The pathologies are well documented and the fallout from them of so serious a nature and so potentially destructive of the post-1994 democratic project that no responsible identity can in any way exclude them (see some statistics below). It is clear, in the light of this, that notions of solidarity and service must be evidenced in the reversal of the various losses.

In more recent years the Catholic Church, in its own quest for identity and self-actualisation in South Africa, has had two major themes shaping its identity. Throughout the later years of apartheid and the resistance to this heresy, the key motto of the Roman Catholic Church was "community serving humanity", a theme adopted in 1989. From this year (2013), and for the fairly long-term future, the theme or motto has become "Community in the Service of Reconciliation, Justice and Peace".

Both mottos, or statements of identity, have been arrived at through processes engaging various sectors: the laity, religious brothers and sisters, people with specialised skills and insights, as well as clergy. Consultations have followed various methodologies, but always with the purpose of reaching consensus and allowing for the "buy in" of as many people and groups within the church as possible. They have been conducted at national and diocesan levels, in each case with as wide a cross-section of people as possible. This, in turn, has become the working material for the bishops as a group, or Conference as it is called technically in our governance structures, to exercise our role as teachers. Again, through numerous processes of clarification we have discerned the necessary identity, faithful to the past but appropriate to the present context.

The process has been one of participation together with the teaching office of the bishops, creatively intertwined to produce a local theology in continuity with the older Tradition. Indeed some have spoken of this period and process as a long-term engagement of the church tradition with local themes!

In the processes leading to both definitive statements of identity, a loose understanding of "theology as praxis" was dominant, i.e. a transformative praxis aimed at changing patterns of oppression and injustice through use of the pastoral circle and deepening a social awareness that is crucial for transformation.

Key components of this praxis which have been features of the Roman Catholic Church's search for identity have been:

- the thrust for a real discernment and disentanglement of a true consciousness and a false consciousness – an ongoing concern or reflection around action; and
- the motivation and practices with regard to sustaining the process of transformation.

The Latin American summary of this position, which has greatly informed our position, can be summed up as "seeing analytically, judging theologically and acting pastorally or politically" (see Schreiter 1986:91-92).

The most recent statement of identity of the Southern African Catholic Bishops' Conference built on this type of foundation, especially on the desire and concern to sustain the dynamics of transformation in the new South Africa, which seems to have hit a vulnerable moment. The Bishops' Conference has highlighted the following five defining features of its public life, saying that it commits itself to working with like-minded groups and individuals to achieve them:

- The development of ethical leadership and responsible citizenship in order to promote the political maturity necessary for the realisation of the common good;

- Using its long experience in education to promote the ongoing development of schooling and education in southern Africa so that all young people may be given the opportunity to reach their God-given potential;
- Striving for a just economy consistent with catholic social teaching so as to redress the gross inequalities in our society and to promote the full and active participation of all in the economy;
- Fostering the process of healing and reconciliation in response to our painful history and to the prevailing tendency to resort to violence in order to promote the human dignity of all in southern Africa;
- Supporting marriage and family life as the foundation of society by affirming the values of dignity, respect, care and just relationships in the family, and by addressing the forces which diminish and destroy it.

As a church we consider that while affirming the best of the Tradition, we have in fact made considerable progress towards developing an understanding of the marks of the church in our context in a way that has moved from a narrow sectarian understanding of the mark of "catholic" as a purely denominational, defensive concern, to one which, in union with people of goodwill, seeks primarily to serve the common good in a time that in some ways is as complex as some of the previous moments of history where definitive understandings of the four marks were moulded.

One thing is clear: before, our realising of the mark of catholicity meant adopting a narrow, defensive, insular position against the world, others and progress. Now it is abundantly clear that we cannot realise our most basic, meaningful identity without others, without those who think differently from us, worship differently from us and outside of the strides being made in intellectual life. Our identities as churches are bound to each other's searches and discernment! We cannot achieve our identity by detaching ourselves even from those who do not believe, but we should always have the openness to dialogue in what Pope Emeritus Benedict termed the "courtyard of the Gentiles" – the meeting place of seekers who believe and who do not believe.

What Harvey Egan has said of appreciating the Eucharist can also be understood and said of the journey into and the realisation of our identity. There are important analogies in it. He stated:

Christians therefore should not understand the Eucharist as a sacral ghetto in the midst of a profane, pagan world but as an explicit coming to awareness of this tremendous drama – full of grace and guilt – that unfolds in the whole of world history, therefore also in our times and in our lives. The Eucharist peaks in that death in which Jesus – in the incomprehensibility of his death – surrendered in total confidence to the mystery of forgiving love, to the mystery we call God (Egan 2006:166).

Statistics

Of course, there are huge social pathologies that frame and impede and challenge the passage of knowledge. Let us not lose sight of the following terrible realities drawn from various sources compiled by SACBCPLO.

- South Africa not only has one of the highest level of disparities between rich and poor, but the disparity also cuts along racial lines, posing the problem sharply. Racial inequality in household incomes is illustrated by the following figures: 25% of households earn less than R500 (US$60) per month, including 22% that are African, in contrast to 3% for coloured, Indian and white combined. The average white household income is six times that of the average African household income. As we saw above, the poorest 40% earn a mere 9% of the nation's income, while the richest 20% earned 19 times that of the poorest.

- 48% of children have a living but absent father. Only 35% of children live with both parents. 23% of children live with neither parent. 6% of children born between 1990 and 1994 achieved a matriculation pass of 40%. 67% of children live in poverty. 35% of children live in households which do not include a single employed adult.

- UNDP statistics show that the standard of living in South Africa for whites is the 24th highest in the world coming, just after Spain, while the standard of living for black South African's is 124th, coming in alongside the Congo.

- South Africa is also a deeply violent society, which is not surprising with a 400-year history of brutality and violence, showing itself now in 177 rapes per day, with over 30% of the rape victims being children. One woman dies every 6 hours, usually at the hands of a partner. Recent figures for a certain age cohort in the old Transkei showed that 1 in 4 males had been raped.

Of course, almost all of these [word missing] are systemic, but that notwithstanding, it points out clearly where the work is to be done and raises questions about why more has not been done and where our contribution can carry more weight. These are the pathologies that rob both the democratic project and our learners of the possibilities of growing into maturity.

Bibliography

Dulles, Avery 2006. "The Church is Catholic". In: Madges, William & Daley, Michael (eds): *The Many Marks of the Church*. New London: Twenty-Third Publications, 43-47.

Egan, Harvey 2006. "The Church is Mystagogical". In: Madges, William & Daley, Michael (eds): *The Many Marks of the Church*. New London: Twenty-Third Publications, 162-166.

Madges, William 2006. "A Historical Overview". In: Madges, William & Daley, Michael (eds): *The Many Marks of the Church*. New London: Twenty-Third Publications, 7-24.

Novak, Michael 2006. "The Church is Catholic". In: Madges, William & Daley, Michael (eds): *The Many Marks of the Church*. New London: Twenty-Third Publications, 48-52.

Schreiter, Robert 1986. *Constructing Local Theologies*. New York: Orbis Books.

The Most Reverend Stephen Brislin is the Roman Catholic Archbishop of Cape Town.

4

THE QUEST FOR IDENTITY IN THE ANGLICAN CHURCH OF SOUTHERN AFRICA

Thabo Makgoba

As I share my reflections[1] on the "quest for identity" in the Anglican Church of Southern Africa, we first have to begin many years before the process that led to the establishment of the Church of the Province of Southern Africa. For this set the context in which Anglicanism developed within this part of the world, and many others: a development that contained within it an increasingly clearly enunciated presumption of the indigenisation of local churches. Inevitably this was interwoven with a similarly long history of tensions around what such indigenisation of local churches should entail. What constitutes appropriate inculturation of Anglicanism, and of Christianity; and what is unacceptable syncretism?

Before I turn to what it has meant to answer these questions within our own context, let me recall some Anglican history. It should be noted that, following the break of the historic churches of the British Isles from Roman Catholicism, the Scottish Episcopal Church (which underwent its own Reformation journey at a time before the creation of the United Kingdom) has always had a separate identity from the Church of England. The Episcopal Church of the USA, which emerged in the late 18th century, was the first Anglican Province outside the British Isles. In fact, for complex political reasons, its first bishop was consecrated by the Scottish bishops, further illustrating how Anglicanism has long had a flourishing life beyond the Church of England.

---

1   This is an edited and expanded version of Makgoba's Archbishop presentation, delivered on his behalf at the conference on 24 May 2013.

By the mid-19th century a growing number of bishops were being consecrated by the Church of England for the "colonies", and a sense of these dioceses having local rootedness grew further. At this time Robert Gray was consecrated in Westminster Abbey in 1847 to be Bishop of Cape Town – a diocese with no fixed borders – and to set up an autonomous "Province of South Africa". He arrived in 1848 and began to plant clergy and churches across Southern Africa, and promoted new dioceses, with their own bishops.

One of these bishops, Bishop John Colenso of Natal, became the main cause of the first ever Lambeth Conference, in essence precisely because of his attempts to indigenise the gospel (though this was just one area of his disagreements with Robert Gray, as those who know the details of this complicated story will be well aware). There were similar concerns about what was happening in New Zealand, and underlying these were broader questions about the extent to which bishops in far-flung places of the world could act in ways quite different from England. It is a little wryly ironic, in the light of more recent disagreements within the Anglican Communion, that it was Bishops in Canada who were most concerned about the extent of autonomy to implement innovations which departed from traditional Anglican understandings and practices, thus raising wider issues of authority and the locus of decision making.

The Archbishop of Canterbury, Charles Longley, was persuaded to call what became the first of the Lambeth Conferences – generally held every decade since – in 1867, though it was made clear that the purpose was only to confer rather than to take decisions. Many bishops stayed away, but those who met passed a number of resolutions.

Resolution 8 illustrates the concerns around the tensions between authentic Anglicanism and appropriate inculturation in the minds of the bishops who gathered:

> That, in order to the binding of the Churches of our colonial empire and the missionary Churches beyond them in the closest union with the Mother-Church, it is necessary that they receive and maintain without alteration the standards of faith and doctrine as now in

use in that Church. That, nevertheless, each province should have the right to make such adaptations and additions to the services of the Church as its peculiar circumstances may require. Provided, that no change or addition be made inconsistent with the spirit and principles of the Book of Common Prayer, and that all such changes be liable to revision by any synod of the Anglican Communion in which the said province shall be represented.

It is worth noting four particular elements regarding this resolution:

- The upholding of Anglican standards of faith and doctrine;
- Yet at the same time, the right of each Province to make adaptions and additions to services to fit local circumstances;
- But that these changes are to be "consistent" with the spirit and principles of the Book of Common Prayer;
- Recognisably Anglican synodical decision-making practices are to be maintained.

These illustrate how the fields of doctrine, liturgy, and ecclesiology and ecclesial polity, were the areas where the tensions between continuity and change were particularly focused. Debates today still revolve around these key areas.

Though Bishop Gray arrived in Cape Town in 1848, it was only in 1870, three years after the first Lambeth Conference, that the Church of the Province of Southern Africa was formally constituted as an autonomous province within the Anglican Communion.

At the level of the Anglican Communion, the questions of local adaptation continued to exercise the bishops. Of major importance is the Chicago-Lambeth Quadrilateral, adopted at the 1888 Lambeth Conference. This was originally intended to be a framework for working towards "reunion" with Roman Catholics and Orthodox churches. But it also became a standard for Anglican identity. It states:

That, in the opinion of this Conference, the following Articles supply a basis on which approach may be by God's blessing made towards Home Reunion:

(a) The Holy Scriptures of the Old and New Testaments, as "containing all things necessary to salvation," and as being the rule and ultimate standard of faith.

(b) The Apostles' Creed, as the Baptismal Symbol, and the Nicene Creed, as the sufficient statement of the Christian faith.

(c) The two Sacraments ordained by Christ Himself – Baptism and the Supper of the Lord – ministered with unfailing use of Christ's Words of Institution, and of the elements ordained by Him.

(d) The Historical Episcopate, locally adapted in the methods of its administration to the varying needs of the nations and peoples called of God into the Unity of His Church.

Thus, its fourth principle became a touchstone for proceeding further with inculturation throughout the Anglican Communion – even though subsequent Lambeth Conference resolutions indicate that not everyone has found this easy to accept in practice. For example, many people would still like to see all Anglicans using the Book of Common Prayer of 1662, which was an effective "cement" for global Anglicanism well into the twentieth century.

The CPSA/ACSA has pursued a fairly conservative path in its liturgical adapation, only issuing "An Anglican Prayer Book" after 1989. This is far less innovative than the developments in many other parts of the Anglican world. This reflects the more Anglo-Catholic temperament that has tended to dominate within our church, not least through the influence of the Mirfield Fathers of the Community of the Resurrection (of whom Trevor Huddleston was a member), through their significant role in theological education.

CPSA/ACSA and South Africa's history

Let me turn now to consider Anglican identity within Southern Africa in the context of South Africa's history. What we find is a "curate's egg" of both good and bad, of both honourable and shameful elements.

The church was not immune from the practices of its South African context. On the negative side of the scale, for example, is the fact that it was only in the 1970s that all clergy were given equal stipends and pensions. Prior to this, there were three tiers of stipends, with only white clergy receiving pensions.

It was only in 1960 that we had our first black bishop, Alphaeus Zulu, consecrated Assistant Bishop in the Diocese of St John's (renamed the Diocese of Mthatha in 2006). In 1966 he became our first Diocesan Bishop, of Zululand. And it was in 1986 that Desmond Tutu was elected the first black Archbishop of Cape Town. Perhaps slow in coming – he had come close, but failed to be elected, in 1981 – but when it finally happened, it was clearly in "God's good time".

On the positive side, many archbishops and bishops opposed apartheid. Famously, Archbishop Geoffrey Clayton wrote on behalf of his bishops to the then Prime Minister, on Ash Wednesday 1957, repudiating draft legislation which would have prevented people whom the state judged to be of different racial groups from worshipping together. "This is not of God" his letter read. He dropped dead in his study (the study I still use) the next day.

Clayton's successor, the rather flamboyant Archbishop Joost de Blank, who was even more outspoken, called the political system "inhuman and unchristian". When he discovered that Prime Minister Verwoerd, who was threatening to act against him, was, like himself, Dutch-born, he offered to resign and leave the country, provided Verwoerd would do likewise!

But apartheid brought other challenges that were perhaps not so well handled. So, for example, in many places the CPSA sold churches in what were designated "white" areas in order to fund new churches in the "group areas" to which so many of their congregants had been forcibly moved. While there were pastoral reasons for ensuring churches were sited where their parishioners lived, it can also be argued that in many cases this practice was little different from acquiescing to the existence of the new areas.

Global and local Anglicanism

Being part of a global family also helped the CPSA in asserting its own identity within the hostile environment that was apartheid. Support came in a range of ways.

These included the solidarity that came through repeated anti-apartheid resolutions passed by a succession of Lambeth Conferences and meetings of the Anglican Consultative Council. In 1983 the Archbishop of Canterbury, Robert Runcie, sent a delegation headed by the Primate of Japan to Namibia, to see and hear for themselves what was happening on the ground, to minister to those they encountered, and to give a report to the worldwide communion. This report led, among other things, to Archbishop Njongonkulu Ndungane (then the Provincial Liaison Officer of the CPSA) subsequently being invited to give evidence on Capitol Hill, Washington. Another example is that a range of Anglican Archbishops, Bishops and other senior figures from around the world travelled to South Africa to support the then Bishop Desmond Tutu and the SACC before the Eloff Commission.

The evolving role that the CPSA/ACSA has played in South and Southern Africa since Robert Gray's arrival, and certainly through the worst years of apartheid and now in the new democratic dispensation, has also been informed and shaped by being part of an historic tradition with centuries of confident political engagement. Before and after the Reformation, British, particularly English, bishops played significant roles within the wider political arena. This has been exercised both in cooperation with, and with stark criticism of, the ruling powers, depending on the issue at stake, and indeed quite often with Anglicans on various sides of any argument.

CPSA/ACSA and "indigenisation"

Questions around the "indigenisation" of Anglicanism within South and Southern Africa arise in various guises. I have already mentioned that, in its language, the prayer book has remained fairly close to its roots (unlike, for example, the Anglican Church in Aotearoa, New Zealand and Polynesia, which in its 1988 Prayer Book draws extensively on Maori and Polynesian imagery). But we have moved to include a number of local figures in our calendar of Commemorations.

Indeed, this has also led to some "reverse colonialism" in that Manche Masemola of Sekhukhuneland, murdered in 1928 by her family as a teenager for becoming a Christian and joining a baptism preparation class, is honoured among the saints and martyrs of the 20th century, with a statue on the West Front of Westminster Abbey in London. Another figure, Bernard Mizeki, a catechist martyred in Mashonaland in 1896, has become the figurehead for African men's groups within our church.

Debate around many cultural practices continues, with a breadth of conclusions. So, for example, offering *lobola* can be entirely compatible with Christian faith where it contributes to the cementing of healthy ties of community between families, fosters mutual respect, and brings dignity to both bride and groom – and provided it does not become a vehicle for greed or extortion. On the other hand, the Synod of Bishops recently affirmed that the practice of being a *sangoma* is incompatible with Christianity. In other areas, such as examining the similarities and differences between the veneration of ancestors and the Christian attitude to "the communion of saints", discussion is continuing. Luke Pato and the late Lubabalo Livingstone Ngewu are among Anglicans who have written on these and other aspects of Southern African cultural practices.

Another example of "reverse colonialism" has, of course, been the increasing adoption of the *indaba* approach to debates within the Anglican Communion, particularly around the difficult issues of human sexuality. The 2008 Lambeth Conference adopted a debating style drawn from the principles of *indaba*. Organisers, of whom I was one, saw in its emphasis on broad discussion – especially among those recognising one another as brothers and sisters in Christ – in which all perspectives are aired in order to achieve a fuller understanding of the issue at hand before then seeking deeper convergences on which a response can be built, arguably had more that was "gospel shaped" about it than the polarising "Westminster model" of conducting debate and passing resolutions.

Contemporary challenges

There is still much work to be done on questions around the Christian faith, which draws on the best of Anglican tradition, and African culture. The tightrope between appropriate inculturation and inappropriate syncretism remains one that it is challenging to walk. The Anglican Church in Southern Africa is also challenged in the continuing evolution of its practices and understandings in relation to the new democratic era. So, for example, we must address the question of how much we can still be "critical friends" with those who were our struggle partners, but who now hold political office, whom we must critique without fear or favour, being unafraid to speak truth to power as necessary. We also have to reconsider what it means to be "salt and light" in these new circumstances, and how to teach our people to be good citizens in promoting a Constitution that provides an excellent framework for promoting the common good, the flourishing of individuals within flourishing communities, which is so much at the heart of kingdom-building. Yet it also brings with it new challenges of pluralism and of promoting a secularism that provides for an equal voice within the public arena for those of all faiths and none (rather than excluding the voice of faith, as do some other forms of secularism, particularly within Europe and North America).

All these are areas where we can learn from our sister Anglican Churches, while ensuring that we apply their lessons to our own circumstances.

In return, we hope that we have something to contribute to them – the particular experiences and lessons learned of how, to a considerable extent, we were able to hold together across all our differences through the years of apartheid. We learnt how to wrestle "eyeball to eyeball", knowing that however great our differences, in Christ we nonetheless belonged together. This is a distinctive feature of Southern African Anglican identity, our history of living – albeit often painfully – with diversity and difference, and knowing how to "fight" one another with the purpose of together finding a closer walk with God.

Thus, to sum up, the quest for Anglican identity within Southern Africa remains a dynamic process. We draw on a wealth of Anglican tradition through the ages, and are in dialogue with Anglican brothers and sisters around the world, as a part of our wider process of seeking to discern Christ's call to us to follow him faithfully, and incarnate the message of the gospel within our own time and context.

Suggestions for further reading

On the Anglican Communion and its embrace of appropriate enculturation:

Chadwick, O 1992. Introduction. In *Resolutions of the twelve Lambeth Conferences, 1867-1988* (ed. R. Coleman). Toronto: Anglican Book Centre.

Makgoba, Thabo [Forthcoming]. "Politics". In: Chapman, MD et al. (eds): *The Oxford Handbook of Anglican Studies*. Oxford: Oxford University Press.

Percy, M et al. (eds) 2010. *Canterbury Studies in Anglicanism: Christ and Culture – Communion after Lambeth*. New York: Church Publishing Incorporated.

On the development of Anglicanism in Southern Africa:

Suberg, OM 1991. *The Anglican Tradition in South Africa*. Pretoria: University of South Africa.

Suggit, J & Goedhals, M 1998. *Change and Challenge. Essays commemorating the 150th anniversary of the arrival of Robert Gray as First Bishop of Cape Town*. Cape Town: CPSA.

The Most Rev. Dr Thabo Makgoba is the Anglican Archbishop of Cape Town.

5

SHOW ME A LUTHERAN

The essence of Lutheranism

Musawenkosi D Biyela

The ecumenical nature of Lutheranism

We Lutherans do not believe that we are the only true church. We are members of one Christian family. The popular saying among Lutherans puts it well: To be Lutheran is to be ecumenical. The church to which I belong, the Evangelical Lutheran Church in Southern Africa (ELCSA), has the following clauses in its constitution under the chapter "Mission of the church":

> 3.4. Working towards the realization of the oneness of the Body of Christ, by

> 3.5. Actively supporting ecumenical movements, and by being prepared to co-operate with other churches for the extension of the kingdom of God, provided such co-operation does not violate the confessional basis of the church (ELCSA).

In compliance with the principle of ecumenicity, most Lutheran churches have an open altar, which means that every Christian is allowed or invited to receive Holy Communion at our altar. We have our dogma concerning Holy Communion, but this is not a reason for excluding fellow Christians. We believe and teach that:

• Christ is really present in the Eucharist;
• In, with and under the bread, there is the real body of Christ;
• In, with and under the wine, there is the real blood of Christ.

Baptism is the only prerequisite. We believe that your faith (and your conviction) do not make a sacrament valid or invalid. The word of God makes the sacrament valid. Those Lutheran Churches with a close communion will exclude even fellow Lutherans from the sacrament.

Via media church

Lutherans belong to a "via media church", which means that we are a "middle course" between Romanism and Calvinism. The "via media church" cannot be monolithic. Lutherans are, as a consequence, not monolithic. Some Lutherans are tilting towards Reformed ecclesiology, while others are tilting towards Roman Catholicism. It is in this context that we must understand Klaus Nürnberger's cry about "Catholicizing" tendencies among some Lutherans (especially ELCSA). Nürnberger (2005:183) says: "Any concessions Lutherans may want to make to accommodate the Catholic position is in danger of increasing the gap between them and other Protestant denominations."

Nürnberger is representing a wing of Lutherans who are leaning towards Calvinism. I also do not think that those Lutherans who appear to be Romanising are trying to ingratiate themselves with Roman Catholics. The Lutheran heritage is broad. What those Lutherans do is undergirded by theological convictions; it is not intended to impress anyone.

Nürnberger (who is also my teacher) is influenced by the Leuenberg Agreement (16 March 1973), where Lutherans and Reformed theologians in Germany reached an agreement on mutual recognition (see Vischer 1998). As a result, there are many mixed congregations in Germany. Most of the Lutheran proponents of Leuenberg are very critical of the joint Declaration on Justification between Roman Catholics and Lutherans, which was signed on 31 October 1999. Their cry was that it will distance Lutherans from other Protestants, as Nürnberger says. It is interesting that Nürnberger's book entitled *Martin Luther's Message* was published on the fourth anniversary of the Joint Declaration (31 October 2005), but it is not even mentioned.

These are the signs of Lutheranism being a via media church. Lutheranism in South Africa is also a combination of plural traditions. As a result there is a variety of Lutheranisms; we host a unity in diversity. There is congregationally based Lutheranism and the Episcopal Lutheranism of Swedish heritage. But this via media which creates plural forms of Lutheranism is an opportunity for making a contribution to Christian unity. As a centrist church we understand all sides.

Let me get to heart of the matter in this plurality: What is it that makes us Lutherans?

The non-negotiable principle

Lutheran churches are confessional churches. Lutheran unity is a unity in diversity. We are united by confessions. There is one non-negotiable principle which unites Lutherans. Every Lutheran must agree that the sinner is justified by grace alone, through faith alone and in Christ alone. Justification is not earned through works, but it is a free gift, which we receive through faith in Jesus Christ. The Fourth Article of the *Confessio Augustana Invariata* (unaltered Augsburg confession) says:

> We cannot obtain forgiveness of sins and righteousness before God through our merit, work, or satisfaction, but that we receive forgiveness of sins and becomes righteous before God out of grace, for we trust in God (Kolb & Wengert 2000:38).

Lutheranism is therefore an answer to the question: How can a sinner be right with God? The answer is three *solas*: by grace alone, through faith alone and on the basis of Christ alone. What informs our faith in Christ leads to the fourth *sola*, namely *sola Scriptura*. Faith is created by the preached word (from the Bible) and is nourished by the word taught and the reception of the sacraments.

The understanding of justification within Lutheranism

St. Thomas Aquinas defines justification thus: "The movement towards justice, in the same way as to be heated means the movement towards heat"

(Fairweather 1954:183). And he continues: "Justification of the ungodly is the consent to abhor sin and adhere to God" (Fairweather 1954:195).

Martin Luther understood it differently. He wrote a treatise entitled *Two Kinds of Righteousness* in which argues that just as there are two kinds of sin (original and actual), so there are also two kinds of righteousness:

> The first, alien righteousness, is the righteousness of another, instilled from without. This is the righteousness of Christ by which he justifies through faith (Lull 1986:155).

According to Luther, justification is imputation of the righteousness of Christ on the sinner who believes in Christ. It is as St. Paul says: "For our sake he made him to be sin who knew no sin, so that in him we might become the righteousness of God" (2 Cor 5:21).

Justification is an act whereby God transfers the righteousness of Christ on the sinner and the sin is transferred to Christ. Luther calls this "the happy exchange" (Lull 1986:603). A sinner who accepts Christ receives the righteousness of Christ. God declares the sinner righteous on the basis of the righteousness of Christ. John Wesley saw this idea of Luther as, in a way, repugnant. He said God cannot esteem us better than we really are:

> The judgment of the all-wise God is always according to the truth. Neither can it ever consist with unerring wisdom to think that I am innocent, to judge that I am righteous or holy, because another is so. He can no more in this manner confound me with Christ, than with David or Abraham (cited in Bryant 1983:141).

I would like to offer two comments in response. The sinner is not invited to believe in David or Abraham, and David and Abraham did not die for anyone as Christ did. This can be a good point of dialogue between Lutherans and Methodists. We can only understand Luther better when we know where he was coming from. Walter von Loewenich (1986:73) comments: "Augustinian order requires two things: absolution love of God and one's neighbour, and perfect humility." Martin Luther felt deficient. He saw himself to be below that high standard. Furthermore, he was tormented by the idea of the righteous God who demands righteousness from humans. His superior, Johannes von Staupitz, instructed him to do lectures on the book of Psalms and the letters to the Romans. In this way, Staupitz was a catalyst for the Reformation (without his knowledge). When Luther started lecturing on Psalms 31:71 and 72, he found the Psalmist appealing to God's righteousness for help. He realised that righteousness is not only God's character; it is also a gift that God is willing to give. And Romans 1:17 made him realise that this gift is received only through faith in Jesus Christ (Von Loewenich 1986:83). This is what led Luther to define justification as God's imputing the righteousness of Christ on the sinner. Luther makes an analogy of marriage in community of property to illustrate his point. When the sinner marries Christ through faith, he/she receives the righteousness of Christ and Christ takes his/her sin.

The second kind of righteousness

The first kind of righteousness is the righteousness of Christ credited to the sinner who believes in Christ. It leads to the second kind of righteousness, our own righteousness. According to Luther, this righteousness shows itself in two ways:

- Fighting against our sinful desire, as Paul says in Galatians 5:24:"Those who belong to Christ Jesus have crucified their flesh";
- In the good deeds toward the neighbour (Lull 1986:156, 604).

The first is what John Wesley calls sanctification. Wesley puts succinctly: "At the same time that we are justified, yea, in that very moment sanctification begins" (Bryant 1983:189).

Luther did not use the word 'sanctification' frequently and explicitly. It is here that the two traditions can enrich each other. The issue of neighbourliness in Lutheranism is inseparable from justification. We are saved to serve the neighbour in his/her needs. I will address the theme of neighbourliness under the theme of *diakonia*.

Lutheran ecclesiology

St. Cyprian of Carthage famously said about the means of grace: "There is no salvation outside the church, for he cannot have God for his Father who has not the church for his mother." In Lutheranism it can said that salvation makes one a member of the church. Those whom God has saved, God assembles. According to Article 7 of the *Augustana*, the church is defined thus: "The assembly of believers among whom the gospel is purely preached and the holy Sacraments are administered according to the gospel" (Walker et al. 1985:82).

The church is, therefore, an assembly of people who gather to share the means of grace, which is the word and the sacraments. The Lutheran church is identifiable through its emphasis on the means of grace and their inseparability. A sermon in Lutheranism is not complete if it does not reconnect the hearer with his/her baptism and invites him/her to the Holy Meal. The Lutheran preacher must preach the word of God in a way that distinguishes between law and gospel. The law tells us what God demands from us; it condemns our sin. The gospel awakens us with God's promise. According to Lutheranism, the promise is the counter-pole to the law (Gritsch & Jenson 1976:44). The gospel is a word of reassurance to the sinner whose sins have been exposed by the law. Nürnberger (2005:147) sums it up beautifully: "The unconditional acceptance of the unacceptable. To preach is to invite the sinner to Jesus, who offers this unconditional acceptance. It is not to threaten people with hell fire.

In compliance with Article 7, every Christian assembly must join the sacrament to the word. The sacrament is the visible word. It is, therefore, important that people be made to see the unity of the word and the sacrament by celebrating the sacrament whenever the congregation comes to worship.

Baptism

Baptism is the sacrament of agglutination. It is by baptism that we are joined to the triune God, fellow believers and nature (represented by water). There is a move now to remember baptism in every service. In the Evangelical Lutheran Worship (American), the service starts with thanksgiving for baptism (see the Evangelical Lutheran Church Book of Worship 2006:169). Baptism does not happen every day; therefore in order for it not to be forgotten it must be mentioned, even if it is not actually occurring. As we are revising the altar book, this will be one of the items deserving attention.

Holy Communion

The Reformers, both Martin Luther and John Calvin, agreed on the need for Holy Communion to be celebrated every Sunday. In his *Christian Institutes* Calvin said that the Lord's Supper must be celebrated at least once a week. And Article 24 of the Augustana says: "We (Lutherans) do not abolish the Mass but religiously retain and defend it. Among us the Mass is celebrated every Lord's Day and on other festivals."

Philip Melanchthon on the same article further argues that: "Assemblies for Communion were appointed by the Apostles to be held on the fourth day (Wednesday), Sabbath eve and on the Lord's Day."

In many places this has become impractical during week days. But we emphasise that every Sunday's worship, if conducted by an ordained minister, must have Holy Communion. The good news is that, with the liturgical renewal evident in many churches, the frequency of Holy Communion is emphasised. William H. Willimon (a Methodist) says: "We might respond to a question: How often our church has the Lord's Supper? By asking. How often should we commune with the risen Christ" (1983:99).

In addition to Sunday, we have rediscovered what was the habit in the early Church, namely that every rite of passage should go with the word and the sacrament. It is desirable therefore to have Holy Communion in a Christian wedding and a Christian funeral. I will not give a full theological reason for having Holy Communion at wedding and funerals. A short statement will be sufficient for now:

Weddings:

* The Holy Communion is a Eucharist, a thanksgiving meal. Since the wedding is a happy day, it is therefore good to have a thanksgiving meal;
* It is important to show the new couple that the means of grace (word and sacrament) are a foundation for a Christian home.

Funerals:

- The funeral is a sad day. Death has struck. The Holy Meal is a meal with a promise, a promise of eternal life. To mock death we celebrate the promise of Christ – eternal life (John 6:47-51);
- Equally important is that those who belong to Christ, both the dead and living (Rom 14:7-9), are together forever in Christ.

Ministry

According to Article 5 of the Augustana, the church must have ordained ministers to generate and nourish faith through the administration of the means of grace (Kolb & Wengert 2000:40). We distinguish between common ministry exercised by all who are baptised and a special ministry (of the ordained). Luther says: "Whoever comes out of the water of baptism can boast that he is already consecrated priest, bishop and pope" (Gritsch & Jenson 1976:72).

He also strongly advocates the specific roles of the ordained: teaching, preaching and administering the sacraments. It is for this reason that Article 14 confines these to the ordained person; the laity can baptise and give absolution in an emergency. Episcopal ministry is a divisive issue in Lutheranism. As Nürnberger (2005:183) points out, there are Lutheran bishops who are in the historical episcopacy, because of Swedish/ Finnish heritage. The constitution of ELCSA concurs that "ELCSA is an episcopal Church".

While ELCSA maintained historical episcopacy, it does not claim that episcopacy is salvific. Therefore episcopacy cannot be a condition that we require from any church in order to have a fellowship with it.

Liturgy

Lutherans are people who follow a written order of worship. Every Lutheran church has an altar book. A Lutheran liturgy is again characterised by unity in diversity. Some Lutherans use divisive terms such as "High church" and "Low Church". This is about how much emphasis we put on the liturgy. What usually divides us are the elements that are "adiaphora".

These are the unsalvific things which are neither prescribed nor prohibited in Scripture. Article 15 was trying to address those things (Kolb & Wengert 2000:48). Eskom used to say: "Switch off non-essentials" – in theology those are the adiaphora. But Article 15 says only that if we think that what is adiaphora can help earn salvation, they become a sin. Luther was very cautious about prohibition or prescription. For him that was legalism. To cite one example, he says: "[For the] Gospel lesson we neither prohibit nor prescribe candles or incense. Let these things be free" (Lull 1986:425).

To be Lutheran, therefore, is to be tolerant. Only one thing cannot and must not be tolerated, i.e. imposing a doctrine of salvation that contradicts Article 4 on justification by grace.

Diakonia – unifying elements in Lutheranism

While Lutherans teach that we are justified by grace through faith without works, we agree that works, as an effect of justification, are necessary. They cannot be the cause, they are just an effect. Article 6 calls the works an act of new obedience. And Article 20 is built on Eph 2:5 and 8, which are about salvation without works. But the author in verse 10 mentions that we are saved to do good works. Diakonia, for me, is the growth of Ephesians 2:5 and 8 into verse 10.

Diakonia is service to the neighbour in his/her need. In Lutheranism good neighbourliness is a consequence of justification. As I said before, we are saved to serve the neighbour in his/her need. Martin Luther's most beautiful words (for me) are these:

> A Christian does not live in himself, but in Christ and his neighbours. Otherwise he is not a Christian. He lives in Christ through faith and in the neighbour through love (Lull 1986:623).

This is a call to engage in diakonia. All Lutherans agree on this element. And there are many examples to show this. Let us cite a few.

- Every diocese in ELCSA has a diaconate director who is accountable to the General Director.

- In many countries in Africa, Latin America and Asia, there is a strong presence of Lutheran World Federation agents to render services to the needy.
- Many parishes have resource centres to help both those who are infected with or affected by HIV/AIDS.

When it comes to diakonia, we do not ask about religious affiliation. We have a presence even in areas where there are no Lutherans. I was at a meeting on diakonia in Montreux (Switzerland); there were a number of Muslims from Asia who were hired by the Lutheran World Service to serve the needy in their countries, which are predominantly Islamic. Through diakonia we broaden neighbourliness to whoever is in need. Our diakonia is not only to offer relief, but we also work with communities to help them to get themselves out of poverty. A good example is the Lutheran Farmer Training Centre in Swaziland. Here we train people in crop raising and stock farming.

The gospel cannot be preached only with words; diakonia is the gospel preached through action. We believe that the church without diakonia is not a representative of the Word who became flesh and dwelt among us (John 1:14).

Conclusion

In a nutshell, Lutherans can be identified as people of:

- The means of grace – Word and Sacrament;
- Ecumenical mindedness. A Lutheran who does not accept fellowship with other Christians is not a good Lutheran;
- Diakonia: we do not do good works for the neighbour to be saved, but we are saved to serve the neighbour in his/her needs.

Bibliography

Bryant, Al 1983. *The John Wesley Reader*. Waco: Word Books.

Fairweather, Alan M 1954. *Aquinas on Nature and Grace*. Philadelphia: Westminster.

Gritsch, Eric & Jenson, Robert 1976. *Lutheranism*. Philadelphia: Fortress.

Kolb, Robert; Wengert, Timothy J & Arand, Charles P 2000. *Book of Concord.* Minneapolis: Fortress Press.

Lull, Timothy 1986. *Martin Luther's Basic Theological Writings.* Minneapolis: Fortress Press.

Nürnberger, Klaus 2005. *Martin Luther's Message.* Pietermaritzburg: Cluster.

Tappert, Theodore 1959. *The Book of Concord.* Minneapolis: Augsburg.

Vischer, Lukas 1998. "A History of The Leuenberg". Unpublished Pamphlet.

Von Loewenich, Walther 1986. *Martin Luther: The man and his work.* Minneapolis: Augsburg.

Walker, Williston 1985. *The History of the Church.* New York: Charles Scribner sons.

The Right Rev. Dr Musawenkosi Biyela is Bishop of the Evangelical Lutheran Church in Southern Africa for the Eastern Diocese, and Chaplain of the Lutheran Theological Institute.

6

THE QUEST FOR IDENTITY IN REFORMED CHURCHES IN SOUTH AFRICA

Jerry Pillay

There are many ways to approach a discussion on the subject of Reformed identity in South Africa. However, in this contribution I shall attempt primarily to focus on the distinctive marks and characteristics of Reformed tradition and theology.[1] What is the Reformed tradition known for and what makes it attractive? I shall also focus on the struggles and challenges that impact on the quest for identity in Reformed churches in South Africa today.

It is important to establish at the very beginning that Reformed identity consists of a number of different strands and each may differ in emphasis in different contexts. Reformation history speaks of a multiplicity of sources, contributions and impacts from individuals and movements. Both forerunners of the Reformation and reformers such as Erasmus, Zwingli, Bullinger, Luther, Calvin and Knox all left their imprint on Reformed thinking and development. This is further expanded by modern Reformed thinkers and theologians such as Charles Hodge, AA Hodge, Benjamin B. Warfield, Abraham Kuyper, Herman Bavinck and Karl Barth. So what matters in each context is the strand of thought which that context tends to emphasise. The point I wish to make is that there are a number of divergent views and emphases expressed within the framework of Reformed thinking and constitution. This can be both an advantage and a disadvantage, especially as it impacts on the issue of identity. Eberhard

---

1   In this contribution I shall stick to the brief of focusing on the distinctive and attractive characteristics of the Reformed faith and not venture into its historical developments in general or in South Africa, in particular.

Busch (2008:207) states that questions about identity only emerge in a situation where identity is not given, or at least not felt sufficiently as the way it should be. If identity is given, then there is little debate about it, but if it is insecure or at least not fixed, the question about identity emerges. Reformed Christianity can suffer the latter condition because of the conglomeration of different ideas, thoughts, perspectives and emphases in Reformed thinking.

Reflecting on the latter point, Busch (2008:207) tends to disagree, stating that "freedom belongs indispensably to Reformed Christianity, also in relation to its own form of Christianity". He continues by insisting that this freedom is a reason for pride rather than despair over the quandary in which the question about identity may leave Reformed Christianity. He further asserts that "freedom is rather a well-considered form of an ecclesial denomination, and the members of Reformed churches may be a little proud of it as a hopeful light amidst the other denominations" (Busch 2008:209). He says this in relation to the concern that the unresolved question about identity should be seen by other churches as a deficit in the Reformed churches. He points out that it is exactly strong identities that keep the churches at an insurmountable distance from one another. The advantage is that the more 'fluid nature' of Reformed churches enables them to have more freedom to enter into the ecumenical space of dialogue and collaboration with other churches and bodies, a point that I shall return to later.

As stated above, Reformed churches do not have just one source of historical origin, even though the Reformed tradition and its theology gets their name from the sixteenth-century Protestant Reformation. This is evidently true in the South African context in which Reformed churches have come from Dutch, Swiss, Scottish and English backgrounds. I have travelled to other parts of the world where I have seen the entrenched, solid and powerful presence of Reformed churches, e.g. in Eastern Europe and in parts of the USA. However, the same is not really true in South Africa or in most of Africa, for that matter. This, in my view, is largely because Reformed churches in South Africa have been planted by different missionary activities and agents. It is these initial settings that have kept

Reformed churches separated in South Africa over the centuries – where the aim of realising a strong Reformed identity has not been at the forefront.

Perhaps another reason that can be attributed to this is related to the political situation in South Africa. It is true that most churches and (even) other faiths were focused on working together in the struggle against apartheid and paid very little attention, if any, on asserting their denominational identity. John de Gruchy observes that after the demise of apartheid churches in South Africa have started to retreat into denominationalism. The quest for denominational identity has become more pronounced and emphatic. It is not surprising, then, that Reformed churches in South Africa have started to work together in many different ways. This quest for unity can be seen, for example, in the (re)unification processes of the Dutch Reformed family, in joint efforts at theological education and training at universities, the working together of Reformed churches on what it means to be African and Reformed,[2] etc.

As these Reformed churches come together, they are starting to realise that although they have been divided by the different missionary activities, as well as by the political, social and economic circumstances in South Africa, they have more in common than they have been led to believe. This, of course, is not surprising since, in spite of the different trends and strands among Reformed Christians, there are certain distinctive characteristics which are common to Reformed identity, experience and belief. So, the question returns: What constitutes Reformed identity? Reformed churches are known for the following features, outlined below.

Firstly, the Reformed tradition is known for its sound biblical and theological teachings, which is not to say that others do not offer the same. I often asked people in my new members' course, as a parish minister, why they wanted to join the Reformed church. The majority always affirmatively stated that it was because of what the Reformed faith taught.

---

2   A conference on this theme saw at least twelve Reformed churches coming together in 2011 on the East Rand. The relationships among these churches continue to deepen.

Broadly speaking, Reformed theology includes any system of belief that traces its roots back to the Protestant Reformation of the sixteenth century. Of course, the Reformers themselves traced their doctrine to Scripture. The classic representative statements of Reformed theology are found in the catechisms and confessions of Reformed churches, e.g. the French Confession (1559), the Scots Confession (1560), the Belgic Confession (1561), the Heidelberg Catechism (1563), etc.[3]

Reformed Christians hold to the doctrines characteristic of most Christians, including the Trinity, the true deity and true humanity of Jesus Christ, the necessity of Jesus' atonement for sin, the church as a divinely ordained institution, the inspiration of the Bible, the requirement that Christians live moral lives, and the resurrection of the body. They have other doctrines in common with evangelical Christians, such as justification by faith alone, the need for new birth (sanctification), the personal and visible return of Jesus Christ, and the Great Commission.[4] Yet, Reformed theology has certain distinctive characteristics in its emphases on the following:[5] *the sovereignty/centrality of God,*[6] *covenantal theology,*[7] *the authority of Scripture (sola scriptura),*[8] *salvation by grace (TULIP),*[9] *justification by faith (sola fide) coupled with sanctification and the priesthood of all believers.*[10]

---

3   For more detailed information on this see Ferguson (1988:569).

4   See http://www.reformedreader.org/t.u.l.i.p.htm (accessed 23 May 2013).

5   It is not my intention here to expand on these theological themes, except to mention them as marks of Reformed emphases and distinction. There is a vast body of written information on these themes that can be consulted.

6   For most Reformed people the chief and most distinctive article of the creed is God's sovereignty. It means that God rules over God's creation with absolute power and authority.

7   Reformed theology has always sought to do justice to the corporate dimension of the gospel. Although the doctrine of grace has generally received the greater focus in contemporary Reformed teachings, covenant theology is the historical superstructure that unifies the entire system of doctrine. For example, it is also used as one of the main points to support infant baptism.

8   Reformed theology teaches that the Bible is the inspired and authoritative Word of God, sufficient in all matters of faith and practice.

9   The acronym TULIP stands for Total depravity, Unconditional election, Limited atonement, Irresistible grace and the Perseverance of the saints.

10   This was one of the most significant points coming out of the Reformation. It means that the interpretation of scripture and ministry were no longer just left

Whilst Reformed Christians may hold these distinctive theological elements, it is true to say that in South Africa they are not used as a basis for separation and differentiation from other Christians. In my view, this is because Reformed Christians tend to connect with other Christians more on a missiological level rather than upon a theological/doctrinal and ecclesiological basis.[11] Increasingly, the view is adopted that instead of seeking to be critical of and judgmental about other Christians, it would be more appropriate to ask what we can learn from them and why are they growing at a rate that one does not usually see among Reformed churches, at least in Africa. The new ecumenism calls for cooperation and learning from one another instead of competition and a refusal to learn new things together. Reformed Christians are starting to realise that they need to submit their own traditions and ambitions to constant reformation by the Spirit as they live as followers of Jesus Christ in ever-changing cultures (*ecclesia reformata semper reformanda* – the Reformed church always has to be reforming).

In such an evolving context we need fresh understandings of Reformed theology and new expressions of Reformed identity. We need to take all that we have in the pool of Reformed theology, tradition, practice and spirituality and embed it in a contextual theology which reflects our current realities, if we are to encourage the revival, growth and unity of Reformed churches in South Africa. There are wonderful signs of hope and life that we must continue to encourage as we seek to "pour new wine into old wineskins". However, whilst this may not necessarily help the endeavour of establishing Reformed identity as such, it directs us to the value of reforming Reformed theology and beliefs, which is an essential principle for Reformed Christians.

Secondly, Reformed Christians place a great emphasis on Christian mission and evangelism in spite of what others may think about the often misunderstood

---

to the clergy but applied to all Christians.

11 This does not mean that there are no attempts to assert Reformed theology and teachings. It describes the general attitude and approach that most ministers and leaders within Reformed churches tend to take. In fact, the accusation is that Reformed leaders do not teach the Reformed understanding of scripture enough.

concept of predestination.[12] It is understood that the purpose of the church is to proclaim the good news of salvation and life in Jesus Christ. It does so in both word and deed. In this Reformed churches tend to embrace a holistic understanding of mission, which includes: (a) propagation of the faith, (b) expansion of the reign of God, (c) conversion of those who do not yet believe, and (d) the founding of new churches.

Drawing from the legacy of John Calvin, Reformed churches believe that the church, as a community, does not exist for itself. It has received a commission; it is sent into the world to proclaim and praise God. It is sent to be a sign, instrument and foretaste of the realisation of God's purpose in Christ for the whole of humanity and creation.[13] The mission of the church is founded on the sending out of the disciples by Christ at the conclusion of his ministry and the empowerment of Christian community for mission at Pentecost by the gift of the Holy Spirit. The church and churches proclaim in the name of the crucified and risen Lord God's saving grace and love for the whole world. In the midst of sin, brokenness, pain and suffering it proclaims to the world in word and deed that God's salvation, hope and reconciliation have come into our midst in the life, death and resurrection of Jesus. It does so in the presence and power of the Holy Spirit.

The priority in mission is God and not church. In being drawn into a common understanding that the church is here to serve God's mission, Reformed Christians realise the significance and necessity of unity. And in the light of this they ask questions as to whether Reformed churches are structured to meet the challenges in the world, or whether they are going on with business as usual when the world around them is changing fast? It must be recognised that many amongst the younger generation of Reformed people are not interested in the Reformed tradition, its

---

12   The concept of predestination has often led to the view that it is not necessary to evangelise, because God has already (pre-)determined who would be saved and who would not. Here, too, it does not mean that all Reformed Christians place the same value on mission and evangelism.

13   Reformed Christians place an emphasis on covenanting for justice regarding the economy and the earth. For example, see the section report (Appendix 14) on this in the *Record of Proceedings: Uniting General Council 2010*, Grand Rapids, (2010:134ff) [there is no full entry in the bibliography?].

confessions and its polity as such, but rather in a church which is effectively and imaginatively addressing the challenges of mission and outreach in our time.

The key interest of young people today is not faith-tradition but faith-encounter. They are not so much interested in the tradition of their parent's church as much as they are in a church that is 'doing' God's mission. They are keen to know about Jesus and what he means for the world today. This is the cutting edge of mission: Who is Jesus for me today? If Reformed churches are to experience revival and unity, it is abundantly clear that they have to ask a new set of questions which relate to God and what is happening in the world. The emphasis in ecumenical fellowship is on the whole inhabited earth: the whole gospel for the whole person to the whole world. These challenges have an impact on the identity of Reformed churches in South Africa, especially as they lose young people to other churches.

Thirdly, added to the understanding of mission, Reformed churches are deeply committed to justice. This is one of the key callings of the World Communion of Reformed Churches. For Reformed Christians, God is involved in all aspects of life. This was a point that John Calvin stressed in great detail in his theological focus on the sovereignty of God. It provided the blueprint for Reformed Christians to be involved in politics and economics and in the transformation of society. It is no accident then that Calvin attempted to create a theocratic state in Geneva. Thus, Reformed Christians were for long accused of preaching a "social gospel" and of bringing politics into the pulpit. This is, of course, no less different for most Reformed Christians in South Africa, notwithstanding the fact that there were some who were on the other side of the political spectrum, for example, the Dutch Reformed Church which justified apartheid. Hence Reformed Christians have influenced and continue to influence politics, democracy and social transformation in many parts of the world. However, depending on where you are, Reformed Christians tend to emphasise soteriology (salvation history) and in other places the focus may be on social justice issues. This is quite prevalent in the different Reformed communities in South Africa. Nevertheless, for most Reformed Christians it is unthinkable to divorce God and spirituality from the everyday experiences of life. This is contained in the two essential beliefs of Reformed Christians: (1) Christians are called to be in the world and not to withdraw from it, and (2) Christians are called to feed the hungry, clothe the naked and visit the prisoner, which sets believers apart from merely doing humanitarian work.

Reformed Christians are actively involved in working for economic justice, gender justice, and eco-justice. Most Reformed churches in South Africa ordain women as ministers, elders and deacons, although this is not really true for all Reformed churches in the world. Through organisations such as the World Communion of Reformed Churches (WCRC) and the World Council of Churches (WCC), many Reformed churches participate in programmes/projects addressing justice issues.

Reformed theologians believe that whilst there is not a separation between state and church, yet in all matters the church should maintain some critical distance from the state. The church is called to exercise its prophetic role in society. These are primarily the reasons why most Reformed churches in South Africa continue to participate in addressing public and societal issues, although in recent times it seems that other churches in South Africa are starting to take a lead in these matters. However, the essential difference is that Reformed Christians participate to transform society whereas, it seems, most Pentecostal and charismatic churches have a passion to 'Christianise' the political and economic sphere.

Fourthly, Reformed Christians are very interested in Christian unity and communion. The WCRC has always maintained that communion and justice go together. They are like two blades of a pair of scissors – you need both to cut. You cannot have true communion without justice and vice versa. At the heart of the Reformation was the intent to reform, revive and renew the church. Basic to the understanding of ecumenism is that the Reformers did not intend to found a new church but sought reform of the whole church. In their minds the church was not standing up to the realities of its time in confronting financial corruption, sexual immorality and political power. Reformers such as Luther, Calvin, Zwingli and the others called for the 'reawakening' of the church to address these issues. In so doing they did not hesitate to point out the inadequacies and corruption of the church which impacted on its life, work, witness and theology. These, for example, are reflected in Luther's 95 theses and Calvin's "The Necessity of Reforming the Church" (1543). This renewal was to have a significant impact on the structure, polity, theology, mission, worship and witness of the church.

John Calvin considered unity to be part of the nature of the church. His fourth book of the *Institutes* is a vivid expression of this conviction: "On the True Church with whom we are to cultivate Unity because She is the Mother of all faithful" (section 4.1). He made repeated attempts to avoid the final rupture with the church of Rome. In particular, he worked untiringly for the unity of the various Reformation churches. In this respect, his assumption was that as long as agreement on the essentials of faith was assured, diversity among the local churches was admissible. The one church consists of several Christian communions that are one in the essentials of the faith and recognise one another on this basis. Reformed theologians persisted in hoping that one day the divided churches would gather in a universal council and confess together the fundamental truths of the gospel.

Over the course of the centuries Reformed churches were at the launch of many initiatives toward unity – both internal and intra-confessional. The hardening of the Reformed tradition into Reformed orthodoxy in the seventeenth and eighteenth centuries and the resulting splits provoked counter-movements. Both in pietism and the revival movements, the quest for unity was alive. The focus on Christian unity is on the agenda of many ecumenical organisations; one of the strongest proponents of this is the World Communion of Reformed Churches. This is explicit in Reformed conversations/dialogue with the Roman Catholic Church, Lutheran churches, Pentecostals and others. We must constantly be in dialogue with other Christians in the interests of Christian unity and witness, and more significantly, because our Lord prayed that "we may be one".

This is an encouraging sign in the South African context, which can also be seen in the work of the Church Unity Commission (CUC). However, in recent times it has been most disappointing to see that after forty years of dialogue, the participating churches decided to abandon the quest for organic unity as well as the concept of Full Communion. Their focus is now on mission and ways in which they can work together.[14]

Fifthly, it is said that to be Reformed is to be ecumenical. Reformed theology affirms the catholicity of the church, stating that the church is catholic or it is not the church. Hence ecumenism is not a superfluous luxury but belongs to the essence of the church. This has, no doubt, been clearly visible in the history of Reformed churches worldwide. In spite of numerous challenges, Reformed theologians played an outstanding role in the beginning and shaping of the modern ecumenical movement (e.g. FF Ellinwood, William Paton, Wilfred Monod and Adolf Keller). The thinking of some Reformed theologians had a decisive influence on the nascent ecumenical movement (e.g. Karl Barth, John Mackay, Lesslie Newbigin, Hendrikus Berkhof). Reformed churches have strengthened ecumenical movements in their participation, desire and attempts to promote unity among churches.

Added to this is the knowledge that we cannot tackle all the problems in the world by ourselves. We need to link, connect and work with other churches and organisations in order to make a substantial difference. As Reformed churches we need to work with other churches, Christians and organisations to address the realities in the world, and this is what we see in South Africa. Reformed Christians also recognise that they may be required to work with organisations that are not necessarily Christian, and with organisations and people of other faiths to address issues of poverty, religious factionalism, reconciliation and peace, education, health, etc. In South Africa, whilst some Reformed Christians may struggle with this, it is true to say that the majority do not, by virtue of caring for the poor, have a problem in so doing.

In some parts of the world ecumenical interest is dwindling and ecumenical organisations are struggling to survive financially. This is symptomatic of the lack of interest and involvement by local churches and denominations. Ecumenical organisations must direct their vision and efforts into mobilising and equipping local congregations and member churches

---

14　There are five churches participating in CUC: the UPCSA, EPCSA, ACSA, UCCSA and the Methodist Church of Southern Africa. The Roman Catholic, Lutheran and Dutch Reformed Churches are observers.

for mission in the world. Over the years I have come to realise that true ecumenism is to be found in the pews and not among church leaders who are bent on protecting their territorial turf related to doctrine, polity and practice. Ordinary Christians are more inclined to work with others to make a difference in the world. Reformed churches need to reawaken to this call and realise the significance of engagement and participation. God calls us to be a community and to work in community to build community. We are not called to be lone rangers on a mission for God. We are called to be God's people working with others led by the presence and power of God's spirit to bring transformation, healing, reconciliation and peace in the world. We do this best when we join with other churches and organisations.

It is my belief that mission happens essentially through local congregations and not in the bureaucratic structures of the denomination. Consequently, for me the future of ecumenism lies in the pews and not institutional structures. If I may to put it another way, the future of ecumenism does not lie in institutional structures which are increasingly becoming expensive and difficult to sustain, but in relationships. The relationships of ordinary Christians with one another, the world and creation are the new emerging spaces for ecumenical work and action. No doubt, such a focus puts pressure on denominational identity but, ultimately, what matters most is our identity in Christ and with one another as sisters and brothers in the same Lord.

Sixthly, the issue of spiritual and worship renewal is high on the agenda of Reformed churches today. This is largely because Reformed churches have experienced conflicts, divisions and splits around the area of worship. What constitutes a proper liturgical style and basis for Reformed worship? The quest for identity and preservation here becomes a driving force. There are some who have left the Reformed church because they believe that its style of worship is not what they prefer. If they desire to effect change, they must leave the Reformed family. This is actually not true about the Reformed church, because in reality we embrace a variety of ways and styles in worship and have the freedom to do so, yet in many local churches leaders are not prepared to think creatively about worship.

In the denomination to which I belong I have come across leaders who are prepared to see their young children and youths go to other churches rather than change the way they prefer worship: loud music, instruments and free styles of praise and singing, and the use of spiritual gifts are simply not welcome. In most parts in Africa, for example, Reformed Christians seem to suffer an identity crisis because deep in their hearts they prefer Reformed teachings, but in the expressions of worship they are more at home with Pentecostals. They love singing, dancing and being moved by the presence and power of the Holy Spirit. The challenge of the "prosperity gospel", healing and deliverance ministries found in other churches impacts on Reformed identity, liturgy and beliefs.

It is true that some of the Reformers, like Calvin, had much to say about worship and particularly about music and singing in church. We need to realise, however, that what was said in their time has to be re-examined in this century. The fact of the matter is that most young people prefer contemporary songs and music, visuals, lights, loudness, etc. It is imperative that we seek to find ways in integrating young people into the church; they are not just the church of tomorrow but, indeed, the church of today. It is okay to change our styles and approaches as long as we are able to maintain the substance and essentials of our faith, and teach in and through all of these mediums. There are many Reformed churches that are providing a balanced worship which caters for the needs and preferences of the variety of their members and are becoming attractive places of Christian worship.

Part and parcel of the Reformed heritage is the stressing of the spiritual disciplines of prayer, fasting and the study of the Word. These are the power bases for revival brought about by the Holy Spirit. For some reason these spiritual disciplines seem to be emphasised less in Reformed churches today. If we are to encounter revival and unity, we need to return to these essential spiritual practices. I have noticed that churches that encourage and exercise these spiritual disciplines are flourishing in numerical and spiritual growth.

As we consider Reformed identity in the area of spirituality and worship we will need fresh expressions in (re)thinking Reformed theology, traditions and liturgy and ask how these impact on global Christian unity and witness today. How do we address these challenges which breed divisions, separation and distinctive identities? What do we say about confessions and creeds, and their use in the quest for unity and mission? We will need to give consideration to these questions as we embrace the new trends in ecumenism and address the fragmentation among Reformed churches, and the quest for Reformed identity.

Conclusion

We live in a day and age when many challenges and contradictions face the Christian church. In order to address these challenges, we are called as Christians to witness and work together as we proclaim the good news of salvation and life in Jesus Christ. In this context we are called as churches in South Africa to continue to seek unity in our witness and mission as we bear witness to the saving love and grace of God in Jesus Christ. I am pleased to observe that there is a greater movement towards the establishment of a single ecumenical voice in this country which includes most Christians and churches, including mainline, Pentecostal and charismatic churches. Whilst we may seek to come together, in such an environment the temptation to assert denominational identity and boundaries may also either consciously or unconsciously increase. My personal view is that churches will not add any value to what God may be doing amongst us as Christians if we fixate on territorial protection and denominational distinctiveness. Instead, we will add value if we offer those distinctive characteristics to the evolving and emerging pool of Christian unity and witness in South Africa and the world. In this regard Reformed churches wish to offer, in a spirit of humility, hospitality and generosity, their characteristic focus on theology, mission, communion, justice, ecumenical engagement, spirituality and worship to the wider ecumenical space. In the final analysis, we do this not so much to assert our own identity as Reformed Christians, but out of a desire to take heed of the prayer Jesus offered in John 17: "Father, that they may be one!"

Bibliography

Busch, Eberhard 2008. "Reformed Identity". *Reformed World* 58:4, 207-218.

Ferguson, SB (ed.) 1988. *New Dictionary of Theology*. Leicester: Inter-Varsity Press.

The Rev. (Prof.) Jerry Pillay is the current President of the World Communion of Reformed Churches (WCRC).

7

THE QUEST FOR IDENTITY IN THE METHODIST CHURCH OF SOUTHERN AFRICA

Peter Storey

Most Methodists would claim to have clarity about their identity, and in some sense that may be so, but the Methodist Church of Southern Africa (MCSA) is experiencing a transition in which the links with its historical and cultural roots are weakening. And because its theological emphases are closely identified with those roots, it is an open question as to how much of that identity will be retained in Southern Africa in the years ahead.

The "people called Methodists"

Some things that Southern African Methodism identifies with include the following:

- A narrative rooted in England, the Anglican Church and the Evangelical Revival of the 18th century;
- An Arminian, "open" theology that has significant social and political, as well as personal relevance;
- A discipline that is meant to produce "practical saints";
- A sociology and political culture that has leaned toward the poor and working class;
- A missionary strategy in Southern Africa that led to widespread growth among indigenous peoples;
- A strong anti-apartheid witness not always matched by internal conduct;
- A multiracial character that has yet to fully penetrate the local congregation.

Beginnings

Methodists identity is tied more to a *story* than a doctrine, beginning at Oxford University when Greek and philosophy don, Rev. John Wesley, in search of more serious religion, joined a small group who determined to order their lives of prayer, study and care for the poor along disciplined and methodical lines, hence the derisive nickname "Methodists". Ten years later he returned from a disastrous missionary expedition saying, "I went to America to convert the Indians, but who will convert me?" Something was lacking in his walk with God. On 24 May 1738, following conversations mainly with Moravian mentors, Wesley had a powerful experience of trusting in and receiving the forgiving grace of Christ. This "warmed heart" event provided the motivational thrust for what became the most extraordinary spiritual renewal of the 18th century. A movement of transformation within the Church of England, Methodism broke away only many years later when Wesley, finding no bishop willing to ordain his followers as preachers for America, ordained three of them himself. What set this movement apart from the more effervescent expressions of the Evangelical Revival was Wesley's conviction that Methodism had been raised up not only to bring an experience of personal salvation, but to spread moral and spiritual renewal to the institutions of England, and especially to offer "good news to the poor" of the land.

"Open" theology and practice

Wesleyan doctrine draws from both Catholic and evangelical theology. It is Arminian, eschewing any limiting of God's free grace, emphasising the "allness" of God's love and the freedom of all to respond to it. The eighty million Methodists around the world have thus been very open to ecumenical engagement and in the 20th century participated in a number of structural church unions, including the United Church of Canada and the Uniting Church in Australia. The Methodist Church of Southern Africa (MCSA) has played a leading role in the Church Unity Commission, the Christian Council of SA and its successor, the South African Council of Churches. It was also a leading participant in Livingstone

House, Rhodes University and the Federal Theological Seminary, both ecumenical ventures.[1]

Wesley never wrote a systematic theology, but his sermons and copious writings make it clear that he viewed all theology as being directed toward the transformation of human beings and society according to the purposes of God. His theological emphases relate to the *ordo salutis*. He had little patience for debating how many angels could sit on the head of a pin, but was greatly concerned with what was required for God to make a saint. Wesleyans see the doctrinal convictions outlined below as central to that process.[2]

Original sin and prevenient grace: This means that we all live with two great realities: our participation in the sinfulness of humanity, making us incapable of truly knowing God, and the touch of God's Spirit upon our lives, making it impossible to forget God. Living in this paradox, even when Wesleyan Christians speak of the lostness of sin, there is a note of hope and wonder because, in Wesley's words, "God directly intervenes in the lives of people, starting them on to the road to salvation." He called this intervention *prevenient* grace, the grace that goes before us, that is there before we are.

Justification by faith and the new birth: Wesleyans believe that there must come a time when the above two realities are decisively reckoned with – when the burden of sin is *too much*, and the touch of God alone is *not enough*. This moment happens when we see that the life, death and resurrection of Jesus is a work of salvation, a redeeming and delivering work, and we place our faith in that work. The part we play is to trust that Jesus has done this work on our behalf. This we call being by "justified by faith" and it radically alters our relationship with God and how we understand ourselves. Much like being born all over again, it begins a new life in Christ.

---

1   The closure, for different reasons, of both seminary enterprises after many decades left MCSA unwilling to again place its future training at the mercy either of other denominations or a secular university – hence the investment in Seth Mokitimi Methodist Seminary, a Methodist enterprise which is open to other denominations.

2   Much of the following material is found in my *And Are we yet Alive? Revisioning our Wesleyan Heritage in the new Southern Africa* (2004).

Assurance: Wesleyans believe that we can *know that it's true*. If in sincerity we take hold of Christ in faith, then we may know with an inward certainty that we *are* God's children. The Holy Spirit witnesses with our spirits that we are the children of God and by God's gracious gift we are able to say "*Abba*", "my Father" (Romans 8:16). This assurance is not about feeling good, but about taking God at God's word.

The universal love of God: The word "all" is possibly the most important word to Wesleyan Christians. We believe that everything above is for all – for everybody; none are excluded except those who desire to exclude themselves. Some may refuse it, but all are offered it, because God *has no favourites*.

These Wesleyan emphases are not original, but they are central to the *ordo salutis* around which Wesley built his theology. Another doctrine remains to be considered, however, one to which Wesley brought a significant degree of original thought, and which he referred to as the "*grand depositum*" of religion:

Sanctification or Perfect Love: While Wesley's "warmed heart" experience was the climax of his anguished struggle to renounce "works-righteousness" – the belief that holiness must come as the result of our own stringent efforts – in the early years he developed a deep mistrust of any extreme form of his newfound trust in the grace of salvation. He could not believe that works had no place at all. How else would one have any evidence of the sincerity of faith if it did not issue in works? How could repentance be genuine unless accompanied by "works meet for repentance"?

Long before Bonhoeffer talked about cheap grace and costly grace, Wesley was saying, in effect, that "salvation is free, but discipleship is not". The gift required a costly ethical response. This is why entry into the Methodist Societies was wide open, but he made *staying* in them very tough. "There is one only condition previously required in those who desire admission into these Societies," he said: "a desire to flee from the wrath to come, but wherever this is really fixed in the soul, *it will be shown by its fruits*." In the words of Randy Maddox (1994), for Wesleyans, "Grace is always *responsible* grace."

Wesley differed from Luther and Calvin by believing that holiness was a real possibility for each human being. For them, holiness could be *imputed*, i.e. by grace God *regards* us as holy, even though we are not. For Wesley, holiness is *imparted*: i.e. by grace God *makes* us holy, where once we were not. For Wesley, justification is what Christ does *for* us, restoring our relationship with God. Sanctification is what the Holy Spirit does *in* us, restoring in us the image of God – and this cannot happen without our full, active and disciplined lifelong cooperation.

What do holiness, sanctification, Christian perfection, look like? After struggling with this question, Wesley finally concluded that, quite simply, it looked like love – perfect love:

> In a Christian believer, love sits upon the throne, which is erected in the inmost soul – namely *love of God and man,* which fills the whole heart, and reigns without any rival.[3]

For Wesley, this love of God and humanity was neither a feeling, nor even a noun, but always a verb. So in 1743 he published the "General Rules", which are the central code of conduct for every Methodist. He wrote these rules to make sure that "love of God and man" would be understood in terms of actions, not merely feelings. They were, essentially:

- *Doing no harm* ... avoiding evil of every kind – and there follows a list of examples that is not as dated as one might think, ending with not "laying up treasures upon earth";
- *Doing good* ... of every possible sort, and, as far as possible, to all people; again followed by a list of examples;
- *Attending upon all the ordinances of God,* including public worship, the ministry of the word, the supper of the Lord, private prayer, searching the Scriptures, fasting or abstinence, and Christian conferencing.[4]

---

3   Albert Outler, *Sermons,* I 3:313-14, "On Zeal".

4   A somewhat watered-down version of the General Rules is to be found in the MCSA Laws & Discipline, Tenth Edition (2000), p. 15.

These General Rules went through thirty-nine editions in Wesley's lifetime,[5] so that every member of the Methodist movement probably had a copy of them. It is as if Wesley was reminding his people that being a Christian was more than how they *felt* about Jesus; it was about a new way of behaving, about joining a disciplined order, about practising new habits of the heart.

The result was that the class meetings became places where simple people – most of them illiterate and almost all of them poor – held one another accountable for responsible discipleship, defined as the love of God and neighbour as summarised in the General Rules.

Because of this understanding of sanctification, Wesleyan theology is "outcomes-based": it refuses to remain a doctrine and insists on becoming a *discipline*, it demands not only believers, but *behavers*, and requires that holiness (i.e. perfect love) be not just a pious hope, but a daily *habit of the heart*. Sadly, the early accountability structures that encouraged such living are much diluted today, although, through the work of David Lowes-Watson and others there are vigorous attempts to revive them through the Covenant Discipleship Movement, requiring participating Methodist to practise *private acts of devotion and compassion*, and *public acts of worship and justice*.

Location with the poor

Methodist identity cannot be understood separately from the sociology and politics of the Wesleyan revival and its outcomes. Wesley located much of his life with the poor and it was in the process of regularly sharing their humble homes, their meagre crust, their heavy burdens and terrible degradation – and marvelling at their courage and endurance – *that he was changed*. This change was no less profound for the future of Methodism than his "heart-warming" conversion.

---

5   This is a point made by David Lowes Watson in his training of Covenant Discipleship Groups.

Like those we now call liberation theologians, Wesley reflected on his theology in the light of his praxis, significantly expanding his understanding of holiness as "the love of God and neighbour". The more he worked among the poor, the more convinced he became that being with the poor was as much a channel of God's grace as receiving the bread and wine at the Eucharist. Wesley became convinced that you could not really be a Christian unless you engaged with the poor of the earth. This relocation of Wesley's soul – this journey downward – explains the progressive movement of his spirituality from piety, through charity, to justice. Holiness, for Methodists, consisted of an amalgam of all three.

This led to significant action against the forces holding the poor hostage. Wesley fought illiteracy by establishing the first free schools, and sought to alleviate the ignorance and diseases of the poor with his medical manual and the first free dispensaries. He saw brewers as oppressors of the poor, helping to make England the first country where alcohol sales were reduced as a result of a religious renewal. He launched the first "Building Societies". He denounced slavery and under the leadership of Wilberforce, a devout convert of the Revival, the slave trade was done away with in the British Empire. Even later, through the suffering and witness of the seven "Tolpuddle Martyrs" – six of whom were members or preachers at Tolpuddle Wesleyan Chapel – the first trade unions were established, empowering workers to achieve some justice in the workplace. The birth of the British Labour party was rooted in Christian Socialism and Methodism in particular.

So Methodism lodged primarily with the working class of 18th- and 19th-century England and, while eschewing the bloody revolution that engulfed France a few score miles away, Methodists became a powerful force for change.

The Wesleyan Christian

Let me, then, offer an attempt to identify an ideal, or "complete" Wesleyan Christian:

> Wesleyan Christians are those who grow from baptism, through the experience of the warmed heart, into lives of disciplined love for God and neighbour, expressed in acts of devotion and worship, compassion and justice, and are willing to be held accountable to this by their fellow believers.

and ...

> Wesleyan Christians take an intentional option to stand with the poor and marginalised in society, against the principalities and powers that hold all such in bondage, declaring the Good News of Jesus by word and deed.

Missionary history in South Africa

Methodism in South Africa was born in civil disobedience. In 1816 the Rev. Barnabas Shaw conducted services in Cape Town for both soldiers and slaves in defiance of the British Governor, Lord Charles Somerset. However, Shaw was preceded by another Wesleyan clergyman who had remained meekly silent for three months rather than offend the Governor, and then gone home. This contrast is a parable of the Methodist story here: on the one hand, championing liberty and justice, especially for the indigenous population, and on the other, often conforming to the dominant culture.

With the arrival of the1820 Settlers in the Eastern Cape, another Shaw, William by name, saw his calling, not only to the settlers, but to the Xhosa people. His strategic vision created a chain of mission stations from Grahamstown to Port Natal, each with its mission house, chapel and school. Multiplication of this strategy made the MCSA the largest missionary and educational influence in the sub-continent, with some 100 000 black scholars in its day schools by 1930 and the Women's "Manyano" the largest women's movement in the land. The MCSA also became the first major "mainline" denomination to elect a black person as its national head – in 1963 – but it took another 10 years before this became more frequent.

Throughout the apartheid years Methodism played a significant role in ecumenical and denominational anti-apartheid witness. Methodist leaders were alongside Archbishop Clayton in the early protests against the "Church Clause" of the General Laws Amendment bill and in every other significant ecumenical action against apartheid. Like the other "English-speaking churches", however, this witness was carried by a minority of clergy and laity, and its much vaunted multiracial character was seldom expressed where it mattered most – in the local congregation. The historic decision by the Methodist Conference of 1959 to remain "one and undivided" in spite of heavy pressure from the apartheid government (and some powerful white members) to split into NGK-like racially defined entities, was a crucial one. In spite of their frustrations, the degree to which black Methodists identified with their church was demonstrated most remarkably when leading blacks from a number of mainline churches met at Hammanskraal to discuss forming a breakaway black "Confessing Church". Methodist luminary Rev. Stanley Mogoba swayed the decision against this by saying, "I'm not leaving the MCSA. It does not belong to the whites. It is the church of my ancestors. Whites can leave if they like, but I will not."

During the apartheid years the MCSA offered a number of significant leaders to both the South African Council of Churches and the Christian Institute. It also launched strong efforts aimed at moving its own people toward gospel-shaped justice and reconciliation. The Renewal Commission of the 1970s, *Obedience '81*, and the *Journey to a New Land* process of the early 1990s each made significant changes to segregated structures and/or negative practices.

The post-apartheid culture of South African Methodism

Identity issues in contemporary Methodism are doctrinal, racial and cultural. While the MCSA is officially "multiracial" and is indeed so in its regional and national structures, on the ground there have always been two ways of being Methodist. What is happening now is an exchange of places between the two.

The MCSA has always been at least 80% black, but when the dominant culture in South Africa was white, the Methodist narrative was determined by its white, "English" history, structures and ethos. Although national and regional structures had been integrated, encounters at the local level between white and black were limited, and until seminaries were integrated in the 1980s, clergy (with the exception of those whites involved in "missionary" appointments) tended to pastor separate constituencies. From the 1980s strong efforts were made to close the local gap through integration of circuits, cross-cultural clergy appointments, etc., but advances remain slow and have taken place mainly in down-town churches and previously white suburbs. Methodism in the townships remains, for obvious reasons, largely black and the rural experience varies.

The 80% of Methodists who were black operated differently. In colonial and apartheid times the strength of the black MCSA lay in its numbers, its strong cultural cohesion aided by a common liturgy used universally, and its uniformed organisations, the Amadodana and Manyano. Despite some endemic problems such as legalism, a tendency to clergy elitism and too-frequent intra-clergy conflict, the witness of the black church through all the difficulties of the apartheid years was strong. Black consciousness impacted strongly on MCSA clergy and a theology of "church in world" was embraced with significant emphasis on community empowerment programmes, political witness, and works of mercy and justice.

And today?

Among white clergy the doctrinal identity of MCSA has been somewhat diluted in the last 20 years. This may reflect an identity crisis among post-1994 whites in general and a feeling of increased marginalisation in a church where the dominant culture has changed. It may also have to do with the hiatus in proper seminary training over this period. A measure of liturgical and theological chaos has overtaken white Methodism. Large numbers of clergy missed the experience of residential theological training and were formed largely in isolation from one another via the UNISA mailbox, with denominational identity being significantly compromised. There is no recognised "Methodist Service", with worship style very much dependent on the individual tastes of the resident minister for the time being. While there are noticeable exceptions, there has been a theological shift to the right, with more white clergy preaching a conservative-evangelical, privatised salvation theology rather than the holistic Wesleyan understanding of personal and social transformation that made the church such a force in the apartheid years. This represents a retreat from identity. Many model their work on the flourishing "non-denominational" independent ministries springing up around them, turning their backs on Methodism's longstanding emphasis on social engagement. White Methodism may be more influenced by mega-church growth techniques than by contemporary Wesleyan theology. Those white clergy who do seek to maintain a holistic Wesleyan witness in the post-1994 MCSA dispensation have their own problems: they sometimes express disillusionment with new leadership styles emerging in the denomination. They are not prepared to play the political game with authoritarian leaders and for that reason also tend to focus on their local congregations to the exclusion of any wider roles, further weakening the "connexional" (co-dependence across the denomination) fabric.

The reversal in the dominant culture has brought the black church out of the shadows and black leadership is confident and assured. At this level there is little sign of the essentials of traditional black Methodist identity being lost. The things that kept black Methodism together in the bad days have come into their own.

However, this is not necessarily good news in the long term: the lifespan of this brand of Methodism is under question, because the very cement that bound black Methodists to each other in the past will have much less meaning for today's "born free" generation. To what degree are the uniformed organisations, for instance, anachronisms belonging to an outdated dispensation from the past? They may continue to have strength – especially in the rural areas – for some years, but what attraction will the distinctive red Methodist Manyano uniform or the red-waistcoated Amadodana have among the future's urbanised, sophisticated, more secularised young black South Africans?

Furthermore, with few exceptions black Methodism still clings to a clergy-centred, pastorally rigid pattern of ministry that ties most clergy to a round of funerals and "sacramental safaris", and brings nothing new to the task of addressing Southern Africa's rapidly evolving spiritual, social and economic needs. It has been said in jest that with their time taken up with endless funerals, often involving long journeys for days at a time, they will need to choose whether their primary ministry is to the dead or the living. In addition, black clergy are fast losing the privileged position they have been accustomed to holding in the wider community. Rapid secularisation is having the same "demythologising" effect that white clergy experienced in the secular 1960s. The search for new, more relevant ways of being church should begin now.

The issue of location also arises: today's black Methodism projects an increasingly middle-class image. Although the MCSA has an excellent history among Southern Africa's traditional rural and township poor, many of those people are now upwardly mobile and, compared with the "have-nothings" of the inner city and informal settlements, they are now amongst the "haves". Ministry in the newly multiracial affluent suburbs, in the crowded townships and rural villages must go on, but right now more than 90% of MCSA's resources are locked into those places, which means that 90% of its ministry is reaching the 53% of better-off people, making the MCSA primarily a church of the "haves". That other world consisting of the millions of struggling human beings in the inner cities and the informal settlements is hardly being touched. Unless a way is found of unlocking resources of finance and ordained and lay person-power, and redirecting them significantly to the places of greatest need, Southern African Methodism could lose it relevance and join the religious entertainment industry that is making such headway in Africa. There is no Godly future in that.

This is not to say that the MCSA is failing to find new, exciting patterns of ministry. The paradox is that while white clergy may feel marginalised, it is in multiracial ministry teams, usually in city and suburban contexts, that the missional cutting edge of a 21st-century ministry is being shaped. The best practice models of outreach engaging the challenges and problems of today's Southern Africa are more likely to be found among such teams and congregations than in traditionally black township congregations, where there is still stubborn resistance to change.

The current MCSA seems also to be ambivalent toward the lessons learned so painfully about church-state relations in the struggle years. The church had to unbind itself from its too close relationship with the powers that be, and white church leaders had to learn to prophesy against their own, then dominant, culture. Because the struggle years forged strong bonds between current church leadership and the post-1994 political elite, they have not found it easy to disentangle themselves. A controversial example in the MCSA is that of one of its ministers is acting as chaplain to the governing party. There seems to be a view that because Caesar is now democratically elected, his DNA has miraculously changed.

There has been little robust theological analysis of any of the above concerns. It is hoped that the new Seth Mokitimi Methodist Seminary will play a part in addressing and hopefully reversing some of the more troubling identity issues in both black and white Methodism. Questions have been raised about the seminary being a denominational enterprise, but if Methodism is to bring anything of value to the ecumenical table, it needs to have some clarity about its own identity.

The most serious challenge to the "new" MCSA identity is surely not very different from the challenge in the apartheid days – indeed, the challenge of the centuries: will the identity of the church be shaped primarily by its theology or by the prevailing culture? That was the fundamental issue in apartheid South Africa, and while the early post-apartheid years seduced many into thinking that the new political era also signalled the dawn of a new ecclesiological and theological day, it didn't take long for us to be disabused and for the default position to be confirmed. South Africa was given an opportunity to be different and failed: the promise of the Mandela era, in which the church was encouraged in its prophetic role, soon gave way to the mediocre, self-serving politics we live with today, of enriching cronies, failing the poor, and attempting to co-opt the churches into silence. Caesar once more has an all too familiar look and we should stop pretending otherwise. Therefore the challenge is not all that different either.

Nobody would wish to see Southern African Methodism conform to its historic past alone. Identities evolve and MCSA is rightly evolving as a church of Africa, but even more it must be the church of Jesus. The most urgent work on identity is surely about establishing the difference between *indigenisation* and cultural captivity or *nationalisation*. It comes down to a choice about which of our identities is primary – our baptism or our tribalism? Sometimes it is difficult to distinguish between them and at other times the contrast is glaringly obvious, but at all times it is crucially important to do so. The arguments for a "Christ in culture" have their place, but wherever the church is too ready to uncritically validate the culture around it, whether in Europe, the Americas, Australasia or in Africa, theology is subsumed and culture prevails. Christ becomes diluted and theology is hijacked by not just the virtues but also the sins of the culture. Catholic Christianity does not embrace any one culture, but remains over all cultures and judges them all. I remain convinced that we are only church – truly church – when Christ is permitted to interrogate to its very roots the culture that has shaped us – whoever we are. We should remind ourselves, in the words of Hauerwas and Willimon (1989), that as Christians we are *Resident Aliens*. Our identity must always be first as citizens and members of the realm of God.

Bibliography

Hauerwas, Stanley & Willimon, William H 1989. *Resident Aliens*. Nashville: Abingdon.

Maddox, Randy L 1994. *Responsible Grace: John Wesley's Practical Theology*. Nashville: Kingswood Books.

Storey, Peter 2004. *And Are we yet Alive? Revisioning our Wesleyan Heritage in the new Southern Africa*. Cape Town: Methodist Publishing House.

Peter Storey is a retired Methodist Bishop and Distinguished Professor of the Practice of Christian Ministry Emeritus at Duke University Divinity School. He is a past President of both the Methodist Church of Southern Africa and the South African Council of Churches.

8

THE QUEST FOR IDENTITY IN BAPTIST CHURCHES IN SOUTH AFRICA

Linzay Rinquest

Introduction

In 2009 Baptists celebrated their quadringentenary. While it may be suggested (tongue in cheek) that Baptist history extends even further back to the time of John the Baptist (cf. Matt 3:1), who was engaged in the activity that came to historically characterise and name this group, it may become clearer through this brief paper that there is more to being Baptist than just baptism.

The issue of denominational identity, from the perspective of social identity theory (SIT), may be explained in terms of the various social identification principles[1] filtered through the "prototypical characteristics" (Ashforth & Mael 1989:20) that inform our understanding of social identity, where a religious group may seek to associate around a common history, a set of beliefs, mission, structure, culture and sometimes politics.[2] It will be

---

[1] Ashforth and Mael (1989:21-22), in using group identification and social identification interchangeably, highlight four principles that govern the formation of the group and what sustains it. These are: (1) a perceptual cognitive construct where the individuals see themselves tied into the collective fate of the group, whether actively or passively engaged in is mission; (2) the collective experience of the success or failures of the group; (3) the internalisation and incorporation of values, attitudes, etc. that become the guiding principles of the group; and (4) a reciprocal role relationship where the individual and group mutually seek "to appease, emulate or vicariously gain the qualities of the other".

[2] For a more detailed description of some of these "prototypical characteristics", see Randall et al. (2006). Fiddes (2003:1-3) prefers to call these "traces" to describe the ambiguity that has often beset Baptists as they strive to be faithful

the perspective of this contribution that the aforementioned social identification principles, filtered through the Baptist prototypical characteristics, adequately serve to describe the main factors that influence the sense of Baptist identity internationally and nationally, and still tend to inform its ongoing quest and struggle for identity. The description of Baptist history (in terms of the SIT principle of perceptual cognitive constructs), the statistical tabulation of the international and national family (within the SIT principle of collective experience), the explanation of Baptist theology (within the SIT principle of internalisation and incorporation) and highlighting of challenges currently facing Baptist churches in South Africa (within the SIT principle of reciprocal role relationship) will form the broad framework for describing the quest for identity.

The historical identity of Baptist churches[3]

Baptists have their origin in the 16th-century Reformation, particularly within the so-called non-conformist or separatist movements within Puritan England (Bebbington 2010:7, 23). While there are similarities with Anabaptism in Switzerland and while some naturally assume some influence of this movement on English separatism, a clear link has not yet been established (Bebbington 2010:29-30). There are various theories that may be proposed regarding Baptist origins (Hulse 1973:v), but the most probable is the one that explains and draws together the various influences which gave rise to the movement, namely "the concept of the succession of principles exemplified in individuals or groups who have held to the essentials of Baptist witness" (Hulse 1973:v). While there

---

to their convictions without becoming too credal as they seek to give expression to their experiences and relationship with God in and through the person of Jesus Christ. Fiddes (2003:12-20) further describes the challenges of seeking to pinpoint Baptist identity, but suggests that there are two ways to approach the challenge. Firstly Baptists could call themselves "baptists" with a lower case 'b' to demonstrate the diversity within the common stream. Secondly, rather than start from "baptistic universals", they could emphasise the "the particular form of Baptist life into which Christ has called a disciple (through many human circumstances) for worship of God and mission to the world" (2003:14), which does not deny the need or desire for local or national associations with the emphasis being on identification rather than identity.

3   Parts of the historical and theological sections of this paper are based on material published elsewhere. See Rinquest (2012).

are also undoubtedly groups that exemplified some of these essentials (e.g. the Anabaptists), it was more the influence of various individuals that provided the bulk of the foundational ideas that collectively came to represent the Baptist stream emerging from the various Reformation river currents! It was chiefly the issue of Baptism that in more ways than one gave rise to the Baptist and other closely related (e.g. Congregationalist) denominations.

The historical origins of Baptists may also be appreciated by identifying the historical seeds of its current theological distinctiveness through individuals who not only stand out as non-conformists in relation to the historical expressions of the Roman Catholic church, but who then also sought to give full expression to these beliefs in faith and church life. One of the earliest seeds of dissent relates to the baptism of infants as exemplified in the non-conformity of Belthazar Hubmaier (1481-1528) as part of the Anabaptist movement in Zurich (Hulse 1973:8; Hoad 1986:53), of which he was a promoter. Hubmaier came to reject infant baptism (Hoad 1986:65) and defended this cause so strongly that he may correctly be termed "the architect of the modern Baptist movement" (Hoad 1986:57). It has to be noted, though, that Anabaptists did not see their rejection of infant baptism and baptism of those who professed faith as an alternative, another baptism (or "re-baptiser" Hunter 1990:14), as the name implies, but rather as true baptism (Hunter 1990:14). While there were many Anabaptist groups that developed extremist behaviours and doctrinal views that modern Baptists would not affirm, these groups where more homogeneous in character in Switzerland, while in Germany they developed a wide variety of expressions (Vedder 1907:145-6). There were also Austrian and Dutch Anabaptists (Hunter 1990:15-16). Like many of the dissenting individuals that suffered the fate of martyrdom, Hubmaier suffered this inevitable fate with his death, for Baptists, representing "one of the purest spirits of the Reformation" (Vedder 1907:156). But it is in the person of John Smyth (exiled from England and the Church of England) that we have what could be described as the "father of the Baptist movement"; when he baptised himself, he started the first Baptist church (c. 1609) in Amsterdam in the Netherlands (Bebbington 2010:32). When Thomas Helwys (c. 1612-13) separated from Smyth and returned to England with a small group the result was the planting of the first general (as opposed to particular) Baptist church in England (Bebbington 2010:38-39). Baptists thrived in England and Wales, fuelled in part by the 18th-century Evangelical revival in England, a general toleration (especially after the Act of Toleration of 1689) and as a consequence of the age of Enlightenment (Bebbington 2010:65-81). It is possible to trace this growth of Baptists to the Americas, but we now trace its specific journey to South Africa.

It was for economic reasons (e.g. the industrial revolution, soldiers return-ing from the Napoleonic wars, etc.) that in 1820 waves of British settlers came to Southern Africa, particularly the Eastern Cape, and introduced the Baptist denomination to South Africa (Hudson-Reed 1977:10; Hoad 1986:209). Prior to their arrival, a small group of these Baptists "formed themselves into a company, and chose as their leader, Mr William Shepherd" (Hudson-Reed 1977:1), with the first services on South African soil led by another member of the party, William Miller, since "they had no minister amongst themselves" (Roy 2000:51). While the first Baptists in South Africa were British, soon German Baptists, who were among the German soldier-settlers (1857) of the Crimean war, added to their overall number, as did other German settlers who arrived soon after them (Roy 2000:51). These groups developed alongside each other, finding it difficult to work together, as they differed on issues such as "open/closed" membership and access to the communion table (Roy 2000:52). Both groups, but more so the German Baptists, were very evangelistic, which soon resulted in a number of churches being formed in what was then known as *British Kaffraria* (the colonialist designation for what is now the Eastern Cape). The baptism in 1867 of JD Odendaal, a Dutch farmer, his subsequent ordination as an evangelist in 1875, led to the founding of 'Die Afrikaanse Baptiste Kerk' in 1886 (Hudson-Reed 1977:20-21). It was in 1877 that the small but scattered Baptist family of churches was formed into the Baptist Union of South Africa (Hudson-Reed 1977:23-24), of which the larger number were German Baptists. A shortage of labour in Natal between 1860 and 1922 resulted in the immigration of about 150 000 Indians as indentured labourers, of which 2% were Baptists (Roy 2000:53). Their request to the Telegu Baptist Home Mission Society resulted in the sending of Rev. John Rangiah in 1903 and the establishment of the Baptist

Association of South Africa (Roy 2000:54). Separate Baptist work amongst Indians was initiated by the South African Baptist Mission Society (of the Baptist Union of South Africa) and led to the eventual founding of the Baptist Mission of South Africa (Hudson-Reed 1983:278ff). It was the purpose of the BMS to plant black indigenous churches that resulted in the founding of the Baptist Convention of South Africa, which has had a tumultuous relationship with the BUSA and led to their separation into separate denominations in 1987. These groups make up the largest (but not only) portion of what comprises the Evangelical expression of Baptist churches in South Africa.

The international identity of Baptist churches

Baptists have become represented worldwide as a result of organised mission, migrations in particularly the 19th and 20th centuries (Bebbington 2010:235-6), the mobility of individuals and families, as well as through literature distribution (Bebbington 2010:243). The exact number of Baptists cannot be known, but estimates are possible based upon those who tend to formally affiliate. The Baptist World Alliance, the most internationally representative body of Baptists, numbers around 42 million members, but about two thirds of all Baptists live in the USA, with a single Baptist denomination claiming around 16 million members (Bebbington 2010:3), namely the Southern Baptist Convention which withdrew its association with the Baptist World Alliance in 2004 for various reasons. The Baptist World Alliance (2013)[4] reports just over 10 million members in Africa, numbering slightly over 70 000 members for the four groups located in South Africa (Baptist Union of Southern Africa, Baptist Convention of South Africa, Baptist Association of South Africa and Baptist Mission of South Africa), the largest BWA affiliate being the Baptist Union of Southern Africa numbering around 42 000. While there are problems with such statistics, they are mentioned here to represent the extent to which

---

4   The statistics for Baptist membership for those affiliated are published on the website of the Baptist World Alliance available at http://www.bwanet.org/about-us2/statistics. The statistics are unfortunately not up to date for some of the conventions. I am aware of some of the challenges faced by a number of Baptist groupings in South Africa as well as abroad in trying to collect accurate or reasonably representative statistics.

the movement has spread. Baptist numbers in South Africa are clearly very small when compared with those of many other countries in the world where Baptists find their presence and a tiny fraction of what is currently reported as the total South African population.[5]

I am aware of other Baptist groups in South Africa that, while not associated with the Baptist World Alliance, do in some way tie into the broader Baptist story and family. These include the Afrikaanse Baptiste Kerke (a general association with the Baptist Union of Southern Africa), the National Baptist Church of Southern Africa, independent Baptist churches that may or may not be associated with the Independent Fundamental Baptist and Bible Churches of South Africa, the Fellowship of Baptist Churches in South Africa as well as the Calvary Baptist Mission Church. Many of the latter mentioned are smaller associations of churches for which I could not find any statistical data.

The theological identity of Baptist churches

While the "Evangelical" label would broadly describe and tend to explain Baptist theological identity, there tends to be a polarisation in this identity (Bebbington 2010:103). Hoad (1986:9) poignantly remarks that "not all Baptists are Baptists". While there are many Baptist groups around the world, as well as those that incorporate the name Baptist,[6] this does not mean that all such groups are necessarily connected historically or theologically to the Baptist non-conformist tradition or ideas stemming from the Reformation in Europe or England. Baptists are a very broad Evangelical grouping that has a number of distinct theological features that are held in common with other Christians. Humphreys (1994:4-22) traces these in terms of at least eleven themes that should be considered the "highest common denominator" because "What unites Baptists and other Christians is far more than what divides them" (Humphreys 1994:22).

---

5   The South African population, according to the 2011 Census, is listed as 51 770 567 http://www.statssa.gov.za/Publications/P03014/P030142011.pdf, which means that Baptists make up only about 0,08% of the population at most.

6   The most notable of these in the South African context is the Nazareth Baptist Church founded by Isaiah Shembe and therefore often called "Shembeism". See Tishken (2006).

Historically, though, some of the unique aspects may be characterised as "separatist, anabaptist and oppose the union of church to state" (Hoad 1986:9). These further developed into the more central characteristic of a "Baptist Identity [which] is defined by this thoroughgoing submission to the Word of God in everything, with the consequent rejection of all else that has no explicit requirement in Scripture" (Hoad 1986:16). Baptist doctrine, which characterises the distinctive features based on this principle, are called Baptist principles, Baptist distinctives or simply Baptist beliefs. But it is the Baptist emphasis on "regenerate membership"[7] that serves as the most fundamental distinctive (Anderson 1989:8) as it is fundamentally connected to the Baptist understanding of the nature of the church. There are at least seven beliefs which ultimately characterise Baptists, which Anderson (1989:8-10) enumerates as: (1) The Christological principle of the Lordship of Christ; (2) The biblical principle of the authority of Scripture; (3) The ecclesiastical principle of regenerate church membership; (4) The sociological principle of democratic polity; (5) The psychological principle of religious liberty; (6) The political principle of separation of church and state; and (7) The evangelistic principle of personal evangelism and world mission. While the international family of Baptists, especially those who are affiliated with the Baptist World Alliance, would readily endorse these principles, it does not mean that there is uniformity on all matters of faith and doctrine!

Challenges for Baptist identity

Theological identities

From its earliest beginnings, even into the present age, Baptists have epitomised variety. There is a popular saying, of unknown origin, amongst Baptists that says, "If there are three Baptists in a room, you will have four opinions!" But beyond this slightly humorous aspect of Baptist identity

---

7   Regenerate church membership has its basis in the Baptist understanding of various Scriptures (e.g. John 3:3, Romans 6:4, Col 3:10, etc.) that describe the personal spiritual transformation of an individual subsequent to a personal faith-based justification, illustrated through the believer's baptism qualifying for church membership. See the discussion at www.baptistdistinctives.org/article9_5_02_05.pdf.

and life is the more serious issue of Baptist theological tensions that often result in polarisation of the Baptist family and spill over into the assumed objectives of ministry philosophy[8] and sometimes results in schism or what is termed "gracious but firm separation" (Aucamp 2011:229). While the particular versus general Baptist issues are only some of those that have plagued Baptists and threatened their unity, it is possible to add a number of other issues that continue to fuel debates that threaten a sense of visible unity and ministry cooperation. These would include the issues of inerrancy, divorce and remarriage, the role of elders, the ordination of women and the social implications of the gospel. The biggest challenge though, at least in my opinion, that Baptists face is in the traditioning[9] of

8   These continue in part along the tradition of the Particular versus General Baptists of the early days of its history in England. But even amongst more "Arminian" Baptists there developed varieties of expression from Pelagian ("belief that anyone who wills to become a Christian can do so") to Xavierite ("belief that anyone who responds to an appeal is, and should be, recognised as a Christian") varieties (Hulse 1973:62). Baptists who tend toward particularism (or who are currently self-described "Reformed Baptists" or "Calvinistic Baptists") will tend to embrace the 1689 Baptist Confession (also called the Second London Baptist Confession) as the standard doctrinal statement (Waldron 1989:425). The main historical purpose of this confession was, amongst other things, to distance particular Baptists from the Pelagian element in Anabaptism and to provide the distinctives of the movement (Waldron 1989:431-432) in a much more detailed format than, say, the 1924 Statement of belief of the Baptist Union of South Africa, but rivals for detail the *Baptist Faith and Message* of the Southern Baptist Convention in the United States of America. These tensions in belief often result not only in the polarisation of constituent churches of Baptist Associations, often driven by individuals (e.g. the "Down-grade controversy" which resulted in the resignation of Charles Spurgeon from the Baptist Union of Great Britain in 1887 (Hulse 1973:30-31) and the expulsion of Norris from the Baptist General Convention of Texas in 1924 (Humphreys 1994:108-9), with many similar issues arising around the world). It is such contention amongst Baptists resulting in "militancy toward other Christians [that] destroys Christian unity. Once the fighting begins, people become suspicious of one another and angry with one another. Militancy destroys cooperation and fellowship" (Humphreys 1994:109). These and other theological tensions within the Baptist Union of Southern Africa often result in individual and groups of churches tending to disassociate, as illustrated in the doctoral thesis of CA Aucamp (2011).

9   At the 2008 Baptist International Conference on Theological Education a number of challenges in ministerial formation were highlighted, including this very specific challenge of character formation. Several speakers from different regions of the world raised concerns as to the quality of students enrolling to be trained for the ordained ministry. There is a lack of rootedness and commitment

its members and new members into its ethos, and which should form an adequate basis for a type of inter-Baptist dialogue that will continue to foster the unity in diversity that has for a large part of its history tended to keep it together.

Cultural identities

Baptists in South Africa have not been unaffected by the political history of the country. Even the four Baptist bodies associated with the BWA have experienced some of the political and cultural tensions that have plagued South African society. While the BUSA has essentially always claimed to distance itself from apartheid, it is well documented that the denomination became guilty of avoiding integration (Scheepers 2008:23, 28) and of adopting a "separate development mentality" (Scheepers 2008:121-2) that had its origins in the British colonial days and became cemented during the apartheid era. It would seem that the Baptist principle of the separation of church and state lead to an apolitical stance that resulted in a "privatised theology of the Baptist Union" (Kretzschmar 1990:30). Hale (2000:226) suggests that Baptists, especially the Baptist Union of South Africa, become guilty of "undeniable accommodation of apartheid cultures". Significant strides have been made, though, in improving relationships between the BUSA and BCSA, with the four BWA alliance affiliates in South Africa having formed themselves into an informal association called the South African Baptist Alliance.[10] While the BUSA has become a multicultural denomination with more than 50% of its membership from "non-white" communities and in its leadership structures, the challenges of full integration remain, with a cultural divide always operating below the surface.

---

of students to the church, and seminarians are sometimes without a formed character within the Christian community. As Brian Harris from Australia put it, "For many students it is not an absence of 'traditioning' in a particular tradition, but an absence of any long-term 'traditioning' in the Christian faith. The matter is compounded because more 'broken' students, with severe baggage, are entering theological institutions to be trained as pastors" (Henry 2008:21).

10 Some of this history is documented in Scheepers (2008).

Postmodernity, philosophies of ministry and the emerging church movement

Like many other denominations, Baptists have been reporting drops in church membership numbers. The same is true for Baptists in South Africa (cf. Scheepers 2008). The BUSA in particular has been experiencing this reality especially in the context of significant gaps amongst younger generations, which seem to be intensified by issues relating to varying philosophies of ministry within the context of the emerging church movement. Many local (more often suburban) Baptist churches report a significant absence of younger people and younger families, who have left for some of the more recent emerging churches that are often of the independent, charismatic flavour. How this phenomenon is to be interpreted requires more careful study, but the reality cannot be denied within the Baptist church experience, especially in South Africa. While there is no empirical evidence for an antidote to such a Baptist decline, the more recent bosberaads and national consultations (documented in Scheepers 2008), suggest that international trends could provide some direction. Murray (2002:1) illustrates this when he says,

> In examining the state of religious life in the USA, researchers have concluded that if not in crisis, it is going through a significant state of transition. Those responding to this crisis or transition have emphasized the pivotal position of that community's charism and mission statement, as a codification of its charism, in terms of its future survival. The value of a community mission is that it is embodied in its membership and manifested in what its members do.

Baptists in South Africa are indeed struggling to deal with this radical transition taking place in culture and have to take special heed of the need to clarify the church's mission. The common adage is "Adapt or die!" While good mission statements on their own will not turn the tide, they are undoubtedly a valuable tool[11] in providing some of the basis for drawing this non-hierarchical association of diverse churches into a unified purpose. It is beyond the scope of this contribution to list and address all

---

11   According to Murray (2002:133), effective mission statements contain four elements: purpose, strategy, value and behavioural standards.

the issues that become symptomatic of this challenge, but the following may be mentioned that would find resonance in most Baptist churches: styles of worship, the challenges of finding a workable congregational polity that provides for effective leadership, the significant inclusion of younger people into active church life, developing the next generation of leaders, and funding challenges for more effective ministry.

Quo vadis for Baptist identity?

This contribution may seem to suggest that being Baptist entails a type of religious schizophrenia! Indeed the Baptist principle of religious liberty and the right to follow one's own conscience seek to facilitate a broad diversity on the basis of an essential unity. It is how broad this base may or should be that could determine the extent to which Baptists would be able to wade through the murky waters of seeking to clarify its identity. The quest for identity should prevent the church from becoming static, but experience would tend to suggest this is contrary to the religious side of human nature, which often interprets change as a threat rather than an opportunity for a clearer and firmer expression of that identity.

Bibliography

Anderson, JC 1989. "Old Baptist Principles Reset". *Southwestern Journal of Theology* 31:2, 5-12.

Ashforth, BE & Mael, F 1989. "Social Identification Theory and the Organization". *The Academy of Management Review* 14:1, 20-39.

Aucamp, CA 2011. "A comparative evaluation and theological analysis of the doctrinal practices of the Baptist Union of Southern Africa, Sola 5 and the Fellowship of Baptist Churches in Southern Africa". Unpublished PhD Thesis, North-West University.

Bebbington, DW 2010. *Baptists through the Centuries: A History of a Global People*. Waco: Baylor University Press.

Dougherty, KD; Bader, Christopher D; Froese, Paul; Poison, Edward C & Smith, Buster G 2009. "Religious Diversity in a Conservative Baptist Congregation". *Review of Religious Research* 50:3, 321-334.

Fiddes, P 2003. *Tracks and Traces: Baptist Identity in Church and Theology*. Colorado Springs: Paternoster.

Hale, F 2000. *South African Baptist Social Ethics: The Captivity of the Church in a Multiracial Society*. Cape Town: South Africa Baptist Historical Society.

Henry, E 2008. "BICTE: A Highlighting of Challenges". *Baptist World: A Magazine of the Baptist World Alliance* 55:4.

Hoad, J 1986. *The Baptists: An Historical and Theological Study of Baptist Identity*. London: Grace Publications.

Hudson-Reed, S 1983. *By Taking Heed: The History of Baptists in Southern Africa 1820-1977*. Roodepoort: Baptist Publishing House.

Hudson-Reed, S (ed.) 1977. *Together for a Century: The History of the Baptist Union of South Africa 1877-1977*. Pietermaritzburg: South Africa Baptist Historical Society.

Hudson-Reed, S & Holmes, RD 1995. *21 Years of Service*. Cape Town: Baptist Historical Society.

Hulse, E 1973. *An Introduction to the Baptists*. Haywards Heath: Carey Publications.

Humphreys, F 1994. *The Way We Were: How Southern Baptist Theology Has Changed and What it Means to Us All*. New York: McCracken Press.

Hunter, D 1990. "The Origin of Baptists with specific reference to Anabaptists". In: Hoffmeister, D & Gurney, B (eds): *Barkly West National Awareness Workshop*. Johannesburg: The Baptist Convention of Southern Africa.

Kretzschmar, L 1990. "A Theology of Dominance: an Alternative History of the South African Baptist Union". In: Hoffmeister, D & Gurney, B (eds): *Barkly West National Awareness Workshop*, 24-32. Johannesburg: The Baptist Convention of Southern Africa.

Murray, Robert J 2002. "Religious Communities and Their Mission". *Journal of Religion and Health* 41:2, 131-151.

Naidoo, M (ed.) 2012. *Between the Real and the Ideal: Ministerial Formation in South African Churches*. Pretoria: UNISA Press.

Randall, IM (et al.) (eds) 2006. *Baptist Identities: International Studies from the Seventeenth to the Twentieth Centuries*. Colorado Springs: Paternoster.

Rinquest, L 2012. "Ministerial Formation in the Baptist Tradition". In: Naidoo, M (ed.): *Between the Real and the Ideal: Ministerial Formation in South African Churches*, 75-90. Pretoria: UNISA Press.

Roy, K 2000. *Zion City RSA: The Story of the Church in South Africa*. Cape Town: South African Baptist Historical Society.

Scheepers, A 2008. "A critical analysis of the structural dynamics operative in the Baptist Union of Southern Africa (BUSA) from 1960-2005 and an evaluation of these dynamics in the light of Baptist Ecclesiology". Unpublished MA thesis, University of Pretoria.

Tishken, JE 2006. "Whose Nazareth Baptist Church?: Prophecy, Power, and Schism in South Africa". *Nova Religio: The Journal of Alternative and Emergent Religions* 9:4, 79-97.

Vedder, HC 1907. *A Short History of the Baptists: A study of the growth of Baptist Principles and Baptist Church until 1900*. Valley Forge: Judson Press.

Waldron, SE 1989. *A Modern Exposition of the 1689 Baptist Confession of Faith*. Darlington: Evangelical Press.

Rev. Dr Lindzay Rinquest is the Principal of the Cape Town Baptist Seminary.

9

MAKING THE INVISIBLE VISIBLE

Women's perspective on the quest for identity in so-called mainline churches in South Africa

Vicentia Kgabe

When the existence of the so-called mainline churches is considered, it is necessary to reflect on those pioneers who established such churches in the (South) African context. In reading the contributions to this volume, there is no doubt that such pioneers were men. A century or so later the mainline churches in South(ern) Africa are still largely led by males. The vast majority of Archbishops, Bishops, Deans, Archdeacons, Superintendents, Priests and Deacons are male. This in churches where 70% or more of those gathered for worship are women, so that women are the most significant contributors to the life of the church. This is recognised by Sue Rakoczy (2004:198), who writes that "these women have been baptised in the name of the triune God, empowered by the Holy Spirit for ministry; however, the power of kyriarchy and the patriarchal nature of the church severely limit the ability of women to exercise their gifts for the good of the church community."

The conference on the quest for identity in so-called mainline churches raised for me the issue of the representation and presence of women as church leaders. Ross (2013:97) explains representation as meaning "when someone or something (an imagery, word, idea and person) speaks about or on behalf of something bigger. Presence, on the other hand, is a much more immediate experiential reality." Because the contributors to this volume (and the conference behind it) were men, the diversity of perspectives that women bring was not represented. Both representation and presence are important and connected. It was therefore proper for the editors of this volume to frown on the absence and lack of representation of women. Throughout the life of the church, the work of women has been immense and vital to the identity of both denominational and ecumenical life. In his reflection on the 1910 Edinburgh World Mission Conference, Kenneth Ross (2009:6) writes:

> The participants were overwhelmingly male, despite the fact that women were already making a massive contribution to the missionary movement. While participants were struck by their diversity, from a longer historical perspective it is striking how limited was their range.

In the other contributions to this volume, historical perspectives on the identity, formation and existence of the so-called mainline churches in South Africa may be found. What is also needed is an evaluation of present missions and ministries, and how these have been and continue to be enhanced by women's ministries. What kind of a church will we be handing to the next generation? A lot is said on the identity of the church, the imbalance caused by colonialism, race, class, language, culture, but too little is said about gender. The identity issues in contemporary mainline churches are not only doctrinal, racial and cultural ... they are also gender related.

The Archbishop of Cape Town and Metropolitan of the Anglican Church in Southern Africa, Thabo Makgoba, talks about the "curates egg" being both good and bad. In his contribution to this volume he states that:

> It was only in 1970s that all clergy were given equal stipends and pensions. And it was only in 1960 that we had our first black bishop. And it was in 1986 that Desmond Tutu was elected the first Archbishop of Cape Town.

I was looking forward to reading the next line, hoping to see him mention that it was only in 1992 that we ordained women to the priesthood and that we were eligible to be elected to the episcopacy. It was only in 2012 that the first woman, regardless of race, was elected to the episcopacy.

This omission highlights that women's contribution to the identity of the church and the ecumenical family is not treated with the same level of sensitivity and acknowledgement as that of men. Ortega (1995:2) writes:

> The church as an institution [with its visible leaders and hierarchical structure, its dogma, canon law and sanctions] cannot escape criticism when its action goes against the fundamental law of enhancing and preserving the equality and integrity of all creatures. All people, women and men, young and old, should feel very much at home as equal creatures of God. All members of the church, the whole fellowship of believers, share a common service of witnessing to the love of God in Jesus Christ and building the koinonia.

John de Gruchy, writes in his essay that whatever else the church might be, its identity is inseparable from Jesus Christ; it belongs to him not us. It is Christ who gives the church its identity. Both De Gruchy and Ortega remind us that our identity as the church is not derived only from the socio-political events at the time when the so-called mainline churches were established in South Africa. Our identity is rooted in Christ, who came so that all may have life and have it abundantly (John 10:10). Women and men have received the charisma from the Holy Spirit. This equality in the Spirit is expressed in Acts 2:17 with reference to the words of the prophet Joel:

> In the last days it will be, God declares that I will pour out my Spirit upon all flesh, and your sons and your daughters shall prophesy, and your young men shall see visions, and your old men shall dream dreams. 18 Even upon (my slaves), both men and women, in those days I will pour out my Spirit; and they shall prophesy.

Rakoczy (2004:215) comments that "thankfully the church is much more than its structures and rules. It is also a mystical *communion* of believers, bound together in the life of Christ Jesus in the power of the Spirit. It is a *sacrament*, a real presence of Christ in the world bringing hope and salvation. And it is especially through the sacraments that the church comes to life."

Elizabeth Schüssler-Fiorenza (1994:167) points out that the book of Acts suggests that women were involved in the Christian missionary movement from the very beginning. Thabitha of Jaffa represents the first stage of expansion, while Lydia is the first convert in Europe (Acts 16:14). God-fearing women of high standing at Antioch in Pisidia drove Paul and Barnabas out of their district (13:50ff), while many prominent Greek women, who were attracted to Judaism in Thessalonica (17:4), and the Greek women of Boroea, listened to the Christian preachers and some were converted. In Athens a women convert with the name of Damaris is mentioned (17:34), while Prisca evangelised in Corinth (18:2ff). Drusilla, the wife of the governor Festus, and Bernice, the wife of king Agrippa, are present at Paul's defence and privately agree with each other that "this man has done nothing to deserve death" (26:31). Travelling missionaries and house churches were central to the early Christian mission, which depended on special mobility and patronage, and women were leaders in both areas.

During the Ecumenical Decade of the Church in Solidarity with Women (1988-1998) a call was made during a seminar on "Women in Dialogue: Wholeness of Vision towards the 21st Century" (held in Bossey, Switzerland in 1994) to the churches to join in envisioning, identifying and acting for a new century. A call was made to the churches to:

- Place women's survival and wellbeing at the centre of their programmes for social justice;
- Give women access to all decision-making power in the church and promote their access in society, working with women to exercise power in non-abusive, non-dominating ways;
- Engage in dialogue and critical analysis of the economic, cultural and political context of each church's life and take appropriate action to combat injustice and to affirm life-giving elements in this context;
- Work to eradicate the abuse of power and sexuality within the church, especially by clergy(men) and other church professionals;
- Review the on-going theological reflection and action of the churches to eliminate teaching and structures which prevent women from living the full meaning of our baptismal equality.

The struggle to realise this hope is the action through which we aspire to live our faith. One wonders how much of the above has been achieved in "mainline" churches in South Africa fifteen years later.

Dana Roberts, speaking at the Edinburgh 2010 Mission Conference, commented that women's spheres of activity in a patriarchal culture are controlled by legitimated space. Legitimated space is space where women are accommodated into certain spheres of activity rather than invited and welcomed (see Cathy Ross 2012:104). The mission field has historically been a legitimated space for women wherein they transmitted and translated dominant colonial culture and its patriarchal structures to colonised "recipients" of the church's mission. So although the many women in mission were defying the cultural norms of their own societies where they were not normally able to preach or teach or have authority in the church, their actions in effect helped to spread this patriarchal culture to other people. From an Anglican perspective, this is especially important for our identity and mission, as it relates to gender diversity. In recent years more work has been done on a variety of levels within the Anglican Communion to question patriarchal structures and approaches, so that decision-making processes now vary from one Province to another and even one congregation to another.

The importance of examining how gender affects the life of the church has been recognised by the Anglican Consultative Council (ACC). The ACC is one of the four instruments of Communion whose role it is to bring together the Provinces of the Communion in terms of information and action. The ACC, at the suggestion of the International Anglican Women's Network, passed two resolutions relating to gender within the Communion. The first was ACC resolution 13-31, which received the report of Anglican Communion delegates to the United Nations Commission on the Status of Women in 2005. The resolution upholds the third Millennium Development Goal of promoting gender equality and empowering women, and asks that the Standing Committee and the members of the church seek ways to realise this goal. The resolution also calls for a study of the place and role of women in the structures of the Anglican Communion.

This resolution was followed by resolution 14-33, which more specifically calls for equal representation of women on all inter-Anglican standing commissions, committees and design groups. Finally, this resolution recommends the implementation of gender budgeting, which is budgeting and budget analysis that takes into account how financial resources are distributed across gender lines.

Nonetheless, the Anglican Communion must still deal with the legacy of the colonial imposition of social norms for gender. Proclaiming the good news of God's reign is affected by who proclaims that, what they proclaim, and who is able to hear it. Gender is woven into the identity and mission of the church.

Bibliography

Fiorenza, ES 1994. *In Memory of Her*. New York: Crossroad.

Ortega, O 1995. *Women's Vision: Theological Reflection, Celebration, Action*. Geneva: WCC Publications.

Rakoczy, S 2004. *In Her Name: Women Doing Theology*. Pietermaritzburg: Cluster Publications.

Ross, C 2012. *Life-Widening Mission: Global Anglican Perspectives*. Oxford: Regnum Edinburgh Centenary Series.

Ross, KR 2009. *Edinburg 2010: Springboard for Mission*. Pasadena: William Carey International University Press.

http://www.anglicancommunion.org/communion/acc/meetings/acc13/resolutions.cfm#s31 (accessed 25 March 2014).

http://www.anglicancommunion.org/communion/acc/meetings/acc14/resolutions.cfm#s33 (accessed 25 March 2014).

Dr Vicentia Kgabe is an Anglican priest who serves in the Diocese of Johannesburg as a Rector of a parish and Archdeacon.

10

THE QUEST FOR IDENTITY IN REFORMED CHURCHES

A gender perspective

Mary-Anne Plaatjies-Van Huffel

The conference held on 24 May 2013 at UWC on "The quest for identity in (so-called) mainline churches in South Africa" focused on the question how ecclesial traditions differ from each other. The question of identity has to do with particularity. This question can easily direct attention to disagreements between confessional traditions, for example, on the Eucharist, baptism, the ordination of women, sexual orientation, instead of seeking to establish common ground between Christians.

The 22nd General Council of the World Alliance of Reformed Churches (WARC) in Seoul (1989) noted in its report on mission and unity that a sense of Reformed identity seems less secure than in the past. The Council emphasised the "community" or "partnership" of women and men when it agreed to appoint a full-time member of staff to address the injustices experienced by women in church and society. As this suggests, the council's concern was not just for women, but for both women and men, for the church as a whole. In 1992 the Programme to Affirm, Challenge and Transform (Pact) was created to promote the full partnership of women and men in church and society. From 1994 to 1997 it organised a series of regional consultations on partnership in God's mission. The 23rd General Council agreed to create a department of partnership between women and men. This department provides a platform for dialogue and action. The department will encourage churches to engage in a lifelong process of transformation into partnership with God, one another and the earth. The 22nd and 23rd General Councils identified some key areas in developing the process of affirming our God-given humanity and gifts, challenging the unjust relationships and transforming gender relations and structures through the gift of the Holy Spirit. It stated: "Awareness of the diversity of the lives, structures, histories and mission contexts of our member churches requires fresh exploration of our common Reformed ethos if we are to speak with a common voice in the ecumenical world."[1]

I believe that the quest for identity has to be understood in terms of the search for a common voice in the ecumenical world. Therefore, the question should be: What is Christian identity? What are we called to be as Christians? The question of Reformed identity is, and should be, a secondary question. Christian identity encompasses any other identities. The word of God continues to challenge the church at large with regard to the misuse of power and inherited institutionalism.

Reformed Christians affirm the five "*solas*", namely *sola Scriptura*, or Scripture alone, as the standard for all faith and practice, *sola gratia*, or grace alone, as the only way salvation is obtained from God, *sola fide*, or faith alone, as the only means that God ordains for justification, *solus Christus*, or Christ's work alone as sufficient to save, and *sola Deo gloria*, or, to God is the glory alone in all things. The five "*solas*" comprise the attitudes, thoughts, hopes and fears, ideals, ideas about the world, life, morality, belief in God, in Christ and the coming kingdom, spiritual practices and ways of organising the Reformed church, and can be seen as the identity marks of a true Reformed Church (see Vroom 2008:191). Reformed Christians also believe in the total depravity of the human race, unconditional election, limited atonement, irresistible grace and the perseverance of the saints. Reformed identity implies an ethos. It is a way of life. Identity, however, is not static but dynamic. The matter of identity usually comes to the fore when people are unsure about their identity (see Busch 2008:208). It seems that this is typical in post-apartheid South Africa. Both in civil society and in the church there is an ongoing search for identity.[2]

---

1   See the Proceedings of the 23rd General Council of WARC, p. 213.

2   See the conference "Towards histories of South African Intellectual Traditions: The histories and life trajectories of 'Coloured' intellectuals", held at the Stellenbosch University, 20 November to 1 December 2012. In popular culture, songs like *Delarey de la Rey* and *Ons vir jou Suid-Afrika* illustrate this trend.

The question is therefore: What makes Reformed theology distinctive? Do Reformed Christians hold to a specifically Reformed theology and confessions – which distinguishes them from other Christians? What shapes the identity of Reformed Christians and distinguishes Reformed churches from, say, Lutheran or Anglican or Pentecostal churches? (see Feenstra 2008:220-223). These questions were addressed at the UWC conference on "The quest for identity in (so-called) mainline churches in South Africa". I will not repeat what was said there about the quest of identity in the so-called mainline churches. Instead, I will concentrate on gender as a cross-cutting issue, which should be attended to in the discourse on the identity of the church.

The notion of cross-cutting issues refers to issues that affect all areas of concern within a particular context. These are issues that have an impact in more than one field. Cross-cutting issues include democracy and human rights, good governance, children's rights, the rights of indigenous peoples, gender equality, a sustainable environment and HIV/AIDS. Cross-cutting issues require action in multiple fields and should thus be integrated into all areas of the church. Gender intersects with race, class, caste, ethnicity and sexual orientation. In the search for identity, the church should place constraints around the engendering of the church, equity and equal opportunity and act upon that. This implies the need for gender mainstreaming. "Mainstreaming" has been widely adopted as a strategy for institutionalising gender concerns within church and society.

At the opening of the first democratically elected Parliament, President Mandela singled out the importance of gender: "Freedom cannot be achieved unless women have been emancipated from all forms of oppression. All of us must take this on board that the objectives of the Reconstruction and Development Programme (RDP) will not have been realized unless we see, in practical and visible terms, that the condition of the women in our country has been changed for the better and that they have been empowered to intervene in all aspects of life as equals with any other member of society."[3] These words suggest the need to transform

---

3   Nelson Mandela, Inaugural Speech, 10 May 1994. See http://www.powerfulwords. info/speeches/Nelson_Mandela/ (accessed 10 September 2013.)

patriarchy in South Africa towards gender equality. The equality of all persons, of women and men, is one of the core values enshrined in the Constitution of South Africa, alongside the principles of non-sexism and non-racism. Everyone is equal before the law and may not be discriminated against, directly or indirectly, on grounds such as disability, age, gender, sex, pregnancy and marital status. Women and men have the right to equal enjoyment of rights and freedoms, including opportunities and responsibilities in the social, economic, cultural and political spheres. Gender equality implies that all human beings, both men and women, are free to develop their personal abilities and make choices without the limitations set by stereotypes, rigid gender roles and prejudices, whereas gender equity means fairness of treatment for women and men, according to their respective needs.[4] Despite having a Constitution that entrenches equal rights, it is so that discriminatory practices, structural inequalities, prejudices, patriarchy, sexism and the social exclusion of women are still thriving in South African churches and in civil society.

Engendering Reformed identity

The access of women to decision-making structures in church and society has improved since the 1994 elections. There is a strong representation of women in both the minor and major assemblies of Reformed churches. The Uniting Reformed Church in Southern Africa (URCSA), of which I am a member, recognises the importance of equitable relations between women and men, the differences in roles and relations of women and men, and how this results in differences in power relations, status, privileges and needs. The church also took note of the obstacles to the full inclusion of women in every aspect of life, both in the church and society. The General Synod of URCSA 2005 encouraged the use of language and policies that support the inclusion of women and men in leadership positions in all aspects of the life of the church. The General Synod of URCSA 2005 denounced the commercial sexual exploitation of women and children through sex slavery, prostitution, pornography, and the trafficking of women and children. Women had been accepted in URCSA during the past decades

---

4   See http://unesdoc.unesco.org/images/0012/001211/121145e.pdf for UNESCO's position on Gender Equality and Equity (accessed 10 February 2011).

in leadership positions as church council members, ministers of the word and even on the moderamen, albeit that theological presuppositions still keep women in submissive roles in church and society. The roots of the violence against women are distorted power relations that manifest in different ways – as violence, discrimination, subordination, justification, and the silencing and exclusion of women from positions of power. I believe that discriminatory practices cannot be redressed simply by the inclusion of women in decision-making structures. They should also be addressed through the deconstruction of the sexist and racist base of our society and the replacement of sexism and racism with egalitarian, non-sexist ways of living.

Since the advent of democracy in 1994 and the emergence of human rights discourse, there has been substantial pressure on civil society and the church to examine their stance on gender equity, and to engage on gender issues pertaining to HIV/AIDS and contraception, abortion, gender equity, homosexuality and same-sex unions.[5] Influenced by ecumenical discourses on gender, URCSA at its inaugural synod in 1994 adopted a gender policy. URCSA has to some extent embraced the concept of gender equity. It has noted how unequal power relations between men and women in the family, society and church underpin discriminatory treatment of those who are not male or heterosexual. Specific themes pertaining to gender discourse that are often addressed in URCSA include views on the relationship between men and women, women in ministry and ordination, women's participation in decision-making structures, ecclesial and religious language, domestic violence, sexual abuse, HIV/AIDS, abortion, sexual orientation, homosexuality and gender-separated organisations in the church.

The presence of women in academic institutions has posed a challenge to the way in which the identity of churches in South Africa is constructed. This is enhanced by the sizable corpus of publications produced by

---

5   The discussion on homosexuality at the General Synod of URCSA (2005), which demonstrated the sharply divergent views on this issue, received nationwide media attention. The report on homosexuality was referred back to the regional synods. To date the issue remains unresolved, as is evident from the *Acts General Synod URCSA* of 2005, 2008 and 2012.

ordained and lay women from different Christian traditions on a vast array of theological themes. These include, for example, contributions by reformed scholars based in South Africa such as Juliana Claassen, Yolanda Dreyer, Christina Landman, Elna Mouton and Mary-Anne Plaatjies-Van Huffel. These women address the challenges still facing churches with regard to the silencing and exclusion of women (see Mouton 2004).

Several women occupy leadership positions in churches. For example, Rev. Dr Elsje Büchner, minister of the Dutch Reformed Church (DRC) Garsfonteinpark in Pretoria, was elected as additional member of the General Synod of the DRC 2011; Rev. Norma Rossouw, minister of Vanderbijlpark, was elected as moderator of the Western Transvaal Synod of the DRC in 2012; Prof. Elna Mouton was appointed Dean of the Theology Faculty of Stellenbosch University (2005-2010); Prof. Christina Landman was appointed as Director Research: Research Institute for Theology and Religion, University of South Africa in 2002 and was elected as actuarius of the Northern Synod of URCSA (2008 to date); Mary-Anne Plaatjies-Van Huffel was elected as actuarius of Regional Synod Cape of the URCSA (2002-2008) and was elected as moderator of URCSA at the General Synod 2012, and as such became the first female to head a church at the national level in South Africa. During the past two decades these women have made an impact on theological discourse on gender and have shaped the identity of the churches to which they belong.

Some Reformed churches, for example the Gereformeerde Kerk in Suid-Afrika (GKSA) and the Reformed Church in Africa (RCA), still question the ordination of women and their inclusion in leadership positions. Such churches are being challenged by Reformed churches such as URCSA and the DRC, with their emphasis on the biblical mandate of full inclusion of both male and female in the body of Christ. Although the official position of women in URCSA is one of equality and full communion, the experiences of many women in the church are often very painful.

In the period from 2007 to 2012 a gender audit was organised by the Pietermaritzburg Agency Christian Social Awareness (PACSA) in partner-ship with South African Council of Churches (SACC), the School of Religion and Theology at the University of KwaZulu-Natal, The Circle of

Concerned African Women Theologians, the KwaZulu-Natal Christian Council and Norwegian Church Aid. The audit covered five churches – the Evangelical Lutheran Church in Southern Africa, (ELCSA), URCSA, the Roman Catholic Church (RCC), the Methodist Church of South Africa (MCSA), and the Anglican Church of Southern Africa (ACSA). Each denomination had to assess the following aspects: a gender policy, a gender desk or equivalent structure, other forums where gender issues are raised, women's roles in ministry, women's roles in decision-making structures, organisations established on basis of gender, church and religious language, directives on issues that relate to human sexuality and/ or women's bodies, and responses to violence against women (see Ryan 2007, 2009). This audit of gender-related policies and their implementation among selected South African churches was later combined with reports from Malawi and Zambia into a single composite report, which was launched at the All Africa Council of Churches (AACC), which met from 9 to 10 December 2011 in Maputu, Mozambique. The goal of the research was to provide a research basis for churches and ecumenical organisations in order to develop policies on issues of gender in South Africa.

The research brought to the fore different perspectives on gender-related issues, i.e. the understanding of gender, structural support for gender transformation, women's ordination and leadership, religious language, and directives on issues that relate to human sexuality, for example sexual orientation, abortion, contraception and condom use. In some churches progress is evident and attempts have been made to widen the leadership base of churches by including women in decision-making boards and committees by intentionally encouraging women to commit to full-time ministry in the church, and to receive theological education. The research indicates that there are relatively few women involved in theological education and formation. It suggests that women are still being marginalised or excluded from decision-making structures in ecclesial structures. Most churches include women in decision-making structures and/or ordained ministry, but very few women are in decision-making bodies where agendas are set. The research also indicates that churches that opened leadership positions to women examined their liturgies and rites over recent decades and rewrote them in more inclusive and simple language (for example, the liturgy of marriage where the language and symbols speak of submission of women). In addition, amendments were made to the pension fund regulations to make provisions for spouses and not only for widows, while gender-sensitive language has been introduced in the church order and in assemblies.

Directives on issues that relate to human sexuality

However, inequality between men and women in the sharing of power and decision making are still apparent in the church. Women have been accepted in leadership positions in both church and society during the past decade, but the dominant discourse and institutional power are keeping women in submissive roles. The inclusion of women in decision-making structures did not change the dominant discourse, however, which has locked women into submissive roles in societal structures. Institutional or organisational power here refers to the way that power is distributed in the church through its decision-making processes. Institutional power also refers to the way that roles are allocated with varying degrees of responsibility: Who is included or excluded in decision making and what priorities are driving decisions about the allocation of material resources in the church? In URCSA women are included in the decision-making structures, but very few women participate in decision-making bodies where church agendas are set and policies are determined. A high proportion of ordained women are employed on a part-time basis.

Conclusion

The church should move beyond the empowerment of women in gender-separated structures. The church should instead include women in church structures and ministry, but should be careful not to merely replace one form of domination and control with another. Churches should acknowledge their complicity in perpetuating sexism and discrimination. They should challenge discriminatory theological formulations and should work towards inclusive liturgies. Sexist practices of exclusion, silencing, marginalising other voices, direct acts, or complicity in abuses of women or children, teachings that enforce submission even in violent homes are all ways of exercising power. The church should therefore mainstream gender in all church planning processes, institutionalise gender-specific programmes, empower women and men, develop ministries based on self-awareness and mutual models of ministry, and create spaces for men to grapple with masculine identity, authentic spirituality, and roles in gender transformation. Cross-cutting issues require action in multiple fields and should thus be addressed in all areas of the church and in discourses on the identity of the church. Mainstreaming requires changes at different levels of the church. A paradigm shift in ways of thinking, as well as in the goals, structures and resource allocations, agenda setting, policy making, planning, implementation and evaluation is needed.

Central to the Christian vision of human life is the notion that every human being is created in the image of God (Gen. 1:26-27, Gen. 5:1, Gen. 9:6, James 3:9). Human dignity is inalienable; it is an essential part of every human being and is an intrinsic quality that can never be separated from other essential aspects of the human person. An inherent dignity is bestowed on men, women and children. In our reflecting on the identity of the church, the emphasis should fall on an identity that binds all Christians together. The church should empower both men and women to challenge oppressive structures; the church should affirm the contributions of people to their churches and communities, notwithstanding their sexual orientation and should address racism, sexism, classism and discrimination both in church and society. In doing so, the church will affirm that Christian identity is more comprehensive than affirming or juxtaposing any particular identities.

Bibliography

Baard, Rachel Sophia 2008. "Responding to the Kairos of HIV/AIDS". *Theology Today* 65:3, 368-381.

Busch, Eberhard 2008. "Reformed Identity". *Reformed World Reformed Identity* 58:4, 207-218.

Feenstra, Ronald J 2008. "Reformed Catholicity and Distinctiveness". *Reformed World Reformed Identity* 58:4, 220-223.

Mouton, Elna 2004. "Remembering Forward and Hoping Backward? Some thoughts on women and the Dutch Reformed Church". In: Weisse, Wolfram & Anthonissen, Carel (eds): *Maintaining Apartheid or Promoting Change?*, 283-292. Münster: Waxmann.

Ryan, Mary 2007. *Audit of Gender Policies and their implementation among selected South African churches*. Pietermaritzburg: PACSA.

Ryan, Mary 2009. *Understandings of Masculinity in the South African Context: Culture, Faith and the Constitution*. Pietermaritzburg: PACSA.

Vroom, Hendrik 2008. "On Being 'Reformed'". *Reformed World Reformed Identity* 58:4, 189-206.

Mary-Anne Plaatjies-Van Huffel teaches ecclesiology and church law in the Faculty of Theology at Stellenbosch University. She is Moderator of the Cape Synod of the Uniting Reformed Church in Southern Africa and President for Africa of the World Council of Churches.

www.ingramcontent.com/pod-product-compliance
Lightning Source LLC
La Vergne TN
LVHW051649080426
835511LV00016B/2571